Scripture

Reflections

of a Christian in the Marketplace

New Testament

Laying Down Our

Work, Family, and All

That Matters Before Jesus

Sang Sur, Ph.D., Th.D.

ISBN 978-1-953167-12-5 (Softcover, Old Testament)

ISBN 978-1-953167-13-2 (Softcover, New Testament)

Dear reader,

This book is published by Prayer Tents Media, a 501(C)3 non-profit Christian Mission organization. At Prayer Tents, we seek to enable Christians globally to form discipleship-focused small groups so that they may grow together while also providing a venue where not-yet-believers may come to see, hear, and feel the love shared amongst followers of Christ.

We need your support. All donations will be used by the ministry to fulfill the call to missions and discipleship.

Please make your donations at:

ptents.com/give

Contents

Prologue – Why This Book?

This book compiles some of the Scripture reflections I had written down mostly over the past ten years. Though many are lost, it seems God allowed some nuggets to remain. These reflections often occurred within small groups. Back in 2010-2013, it was within a ministry setting, along with some committed members. Beyond that, I took part in other small groups and shared Scripture reflections as a member. At times, I just saved the notes for myself, as I felt led for future reference. I share these reflections with you for a couple of reasons:

1. I want to encourage you, Christian brother or sister, to do the same, especially if you are called to the marketplace as a professional or a business owner. I realized as I read through a decade of Scripture reflections that:

   a. I held the same core beliefs while adjusting in my approach to them. Without the ability to reflect on myself from ten years ago, I thought perhaps my current way of thinking is the revised me, only developed through recent influences and thinking. Yet, it showed me that God's calling and His rendering of my heart began long ago. It was not a new thought that I picked up over trends, but something God had placed in my heart as a calling in my life.

   The same may be for you. You may have lost or forgotten about what God had placed in your heart. So I want to encourage you to read the Scriptures and write down what God shares with you today.

   b. I have been growing in my faith. The things I wrote about many years ago that I never believed could be possible *had been done* but was forgotten.

By writing down your reflections and what God tells you helps you to see how far you have grown and what God has accomplished during your lifetime.

There were also times when I laughed, wondering how I thought so small and wrote in a blue tone when God had so much more prepared for me, which connects to the next point.

c. Who is the best person who can you kick you out of discouragement and despair? You can!

Often, the reflections were written down when things were going well, and I felt close to the Lord. When situations change, and I may feel spiritually dry, the encouragements and exhortations I wrote strengthened me the most. Refreshing occurs because the person writes with the same experiences and vision of the reader despite the new circumstances s/he may be experiencing. Though I may feel discouraged today, there is a person who speaks the same heart that I had and pushes me on toward living out my life for Jesus. His recommendations seem right on. It will feel the same for you.

I may not be able to get the same when looking through writings or reflections written by other people because these reflections are personal, and everyone's calling is unique.

d. Additionally, there were many aha moments where I realized how much zeal I had years ago; and a part of me is jealous of that zeal and want to revive that part in me!

And so, my brother or sister, I encourage you to do the same and write down your Scripture reflections for your future self to keep you as you draw closer to accomplishing your destiny, as more difficult trials may come.

2. I want to encourage you to do this in a small group. Read a chapter a day together with close-knit brothers and sisters and share your favorite verses. It is ok not to have any commentary at all times, but just a simple, "I like that verse," will encourage other members of your group to keep going and growing in Christ. If you were to write down your reflections just once a week, you would have 52 each year. As you make this a practice, especially with others, you may end up with more than that each year.

3. I want to introduce Prayer Tents. It is a Christian mission organization that desires to enable discipleship around the world. Jesus called all His followers, you and me, to make disciples. Yet, to make them, we must be one ourselves. To be a disciple, it requires small groups that commit to life-on-life growth together.

   Prayer Tents seeks to enable and support discipleship-in-Christ-focused small groups. One of the ways is to make it easy to read the Scriptures, to save the verses you like, and share them with your small group members.

   Make use of Prayer Tents to save your Scripture reflections. Share them with your small group to encourage them daily or privately just for your future self. This book is only an example of what you can do too.

4. For many years, I had lay responsibilities to lead young adult groups, ages 18-39 (see *to1another.com* for an explanation of that age group) while still working in the corporate world. Even though I have received ordination over time, it is for a special purpose, and I recognize God's calling for me is in the marketplace. I am no different from you, who may be called to the marketplace as well.

I share this to say, if you are a person called to the marketplace, *you must reflect on the Scriptures too.* You are called to make disciples. You are called to be a missionary. You are called to be a tentmaker and a leader in the marketplace. God has made you so that you can form relationships, perhaps deeper than what a pastor may be able. You have the influence of a king to attract people to Christ by the way you live. How can you do this? Be a disciple of Jesus and go deep into the Word of God. Scripture is your lifeline, just as it is for all followers of Jesus. Now, make it count by making it your foundation and sharing it to encourage others.

Consider how David made his business decisions. He asked God, "Should I move back to one of the towns of Judah?" God answered, "Yes." To which town? Hebron. As leaders in the marketplace, we need to dialogue like this with God in all our decisions. People around us will see the wisdom in our actions and fruitfulness of our pursuits because the Lord is with us. (See reflection #137 for the Scripture reference and the full story of how David became king).

It is through your knowledge of Scriptures that you can discern when He calls. It is through your Scripture reflections that you will hear His voice amidst many others, especially as we must make timely decisions and act.

So, kings, go deep into the Word of God and live your life with full trust in Him. It is through your deep reflections in Scriptures that you can draw close to God and hear Him. It is how you will complete your God-given destiny and fulfill your calling.

Your Fellow Brother in Christ,

Dr. Sang Sur

How to Use This Book

Use this book in various ways:

1. **For yourself.**

   Pick a number, go sequentially, or pick a book of the Bible to begin your reflections.

   If possible, read the entire chapter of the Scriptures from the reflection (go to prayertents.com for easy access to Scriptures or get the app. It works well when all small group members use it.), or if time does not permit it, read the verses provided for each reflection.

   Reflect on what the passage says. What is God saying to you? Then read the author's writing and prayerfully consider what God is doing, wants you to do, or be still and listen. You may also dialogue over the feelings that the Holy Spirit is giving you and ask questions.

   Draw close to Him and trust Him for the rest of your day, and keep coming back for further reflections.

   Store your reflections on Prayer Tents so that you can have a record of your current thinking for future review (see next section on how to do that).

2. **For your small group. Use this as a way to build conversations.**

   Pick one or a few numbers together, or pick a book of the Bible.

   Just as when you would reflect personally following the directions from above, read through the Scriptures together then the author's reflections. Upon each, share with one another what God may be telling you or where He may be leading you. Also, draw some questions that may have arisen from your readings and reflections, especially on what you experience in your living, including within the family, work, church, or any other relationships.

Also, ask God together for the next steps.

May it be a powerful time of God coming down in power and transforming every group member.

3. **As an idea template to help your group to grow in discipleship.**

Use the Scripture reflections as examples and template to encourage your group to start building your own Scripture reflections together. Encourage one another to read Scriptures daily and share how God is leading you. Again, prayertents.com may be helpful to you to store your reflections and share with one another while helping you keep track of the chapters to read each day.

How to record your Scripture Reflection on Prayer Tents

1. On your mobile device, download the "Prayer Tents" app on Android or iOS. Then login at prayertents.com. (You must be logged in to save your notes)

2. Select the section of Scripture you wish to read

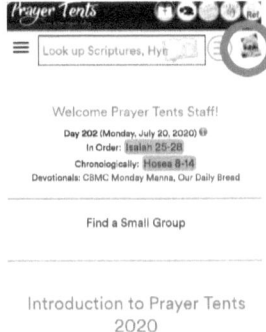 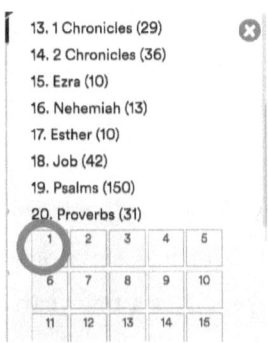

3. Select a verse (or verses) you liked then click on the "like" symbol. Then on the next screen "add notes." Type in your reflections and hit "publish." (Note: you can make it private so no one else can see your notes.)

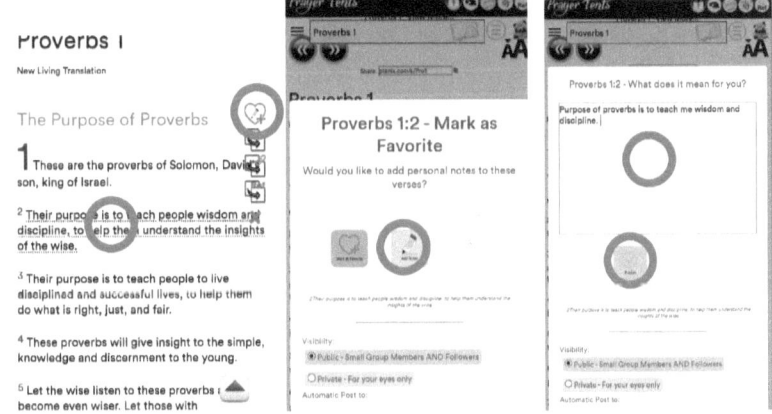

4. You can review your notes and edit them by visiting your notes page.

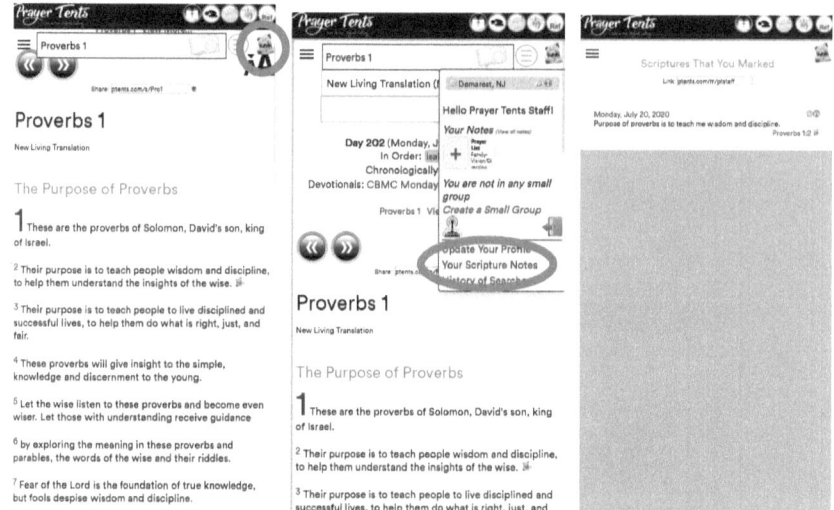

5. And that's it. Keep doing this daily. Do it with your small groups. After a few years, review your reflections to see how much your life has changed as a result of your focus on Scriptures.

Matthew

314.

> Herod was furious when he realized that the
> wise men had outwitted him. He sent soldiers to
> kill all the boys in and around Bethlehem who
> were two years old and under, based on the wise
> men's report of the star's first appearance.

Matthew 2:16

God's plans are always fulfilled. His divine providence and protection is there. Being aligned with God's will means that opposing/competing activities can be frustrated while we find success in our obedience to God's calling.

#godprovides #godhasaplan #godisfaithful #godisable #godisforus #trustgod #waitongod #calling #bedifferent

Thursday, October 3, 2019, New York, NY

315.

> Jesus traveled throughout the region of Galilee,
> teaching in the synagogues and announcing the
> Good News about the Kingdom. And he healed
> every kind of disease and illness.

Matthew 4:23

People followed Him.

They were genuinely interested in hearing more. It says Jesus did two things: 1. He taught and 2. healed.

We too, let us not be afraid to speak up and to perform miracles including healing.

We must be a people of influence who people would want to follow.

We do not want people to follow because we are so good, but because the God we serve is SOOOO good. That can happen when we do these two things: teach about Him and demonstrate God's love through miracles.

#letyourlifeshine #trustgod #calling #walkinfaith #wearethechurch #bedifferent #makegodpriority #visionary

Saturday, April 11, 2020, Old Tappan, NJ USA

316.

One day as he saw the crowds gathering, Jesus went up on the mountainside and sat down. His disciples gathered around him, and he began to teach them.

Matthew 5:1-2

Some people are looking for teaching to help them with their struggles. We need to grow in influence so that people would want to hear and also grow in righteousness, living in the right way especially toward others, so that we may have an opportunity to teach them.

#bedifferent #meaningfullife #calling #honorgod #letyourlifeshine #walkwithgod #blessothers

Sunday, October 6, 2019, New York, NY

317.

Give your gifts in private, and your Father, who
sees everything, will reward you. But when you
pray, go away by yourself, shut the door behind
you, and pray to your Father in private. Then
your Father, who sees everything, will reward
you. Then no one will notice that you are fasting,
except your Father, who knows what you do in
private. And your Father, who sees everything,
will reward you.

Matthew 6:4,6,18

Give in private, without showing others.

I would also add, do the things that make you busy in private,
while in front of others, be available.

#loveothers #blessothers #bedifferent #letyourlifeshine #visionary #relationshipsmatter

Monday, October 7, 2019, New York, NY

318.

Suddenly, a man with leprosy approached him
and knelt before him. "Lord," the man said, "if
you are willing, you can heal me and make me
clean."

Matthew 8:2

Jesus, if you are willing…

This chapter shows that there is nothing impossible for God.
This can refer to our physical sicknesses, but also fruitfulness of our
businesses, profession, our families, and our successes. God can restore
anything. When the leper said to Jesus, "if you are willing," Jesus replied,
"I am willing." Our God is for us.

For healing and restoration, there are two components:

1. God's will, not our own. We can certainly ask and see where God leads us.

2. Willingness to believe and obey (see verse 22). It requires faith on our part.

#heartmatters #letgoletgod #walkinfaith #breakthrough #notofthisworld #nothingisimpossiblewithgod

Wednesday, October 9, 2019, New York, NY

319.

> As Jesus was walking along, he saw a man named Matthew sitting at his tax collector's booth. "Follow me and be my disciple," Jesus said to him. So Matthew got up and followed him. They went right into the house where he was staying, and Jesus asked them, "Do you believe I can make you see?" "Yes, Lord," they told him, "we do."
>
> Matthew 9:28

People are waiting to follow someone. When that person comes and asks to follow, they may drop what they have been doing, which is often "just a job" or something they had to do to make a living, and follow.

As business leaders, we must become influential and inspire people to greater things so that 1. They would follow, then 2. They would see, do, and believe in greater things because of us.

When Jesus asks us to follow, the question that we must answer is, "do you believe God can do _____ for you?" The blank may be "make the business flourish," "bring your family back together," or "give greater insight." If you can answer yes, that is when God can make that happen. Opposite of this would be uncertainty, doubt, and trust in self—own abilities, education, and experiences.

Let us depend on God so He can lead our lives and all things around it.

#gowhengodcalls #submittogod #godhasaplan #godusesregularpeople #makegodpriority #godrestores

Thursday, October 10, 2019, New York, NY

320.

> But some Pharisees saw them do it and protested, "Look, your disciples are breaking the law by harvesting grain on the Sabbath."

> Matthew 12:2

If people want to find fault, they will. It is interesting how Pharisees tried to nitpick an accusation toward someone who was hungry and ate as someone that "harvested" and worked.

We matter more to God than following rules.

He wants us to eat when we are hungry, be healed when we are sick, and wants us to rest (have sabbath) from the busyness of the world.

Have a wonderful day of rest everyone!

#letyourlifeshine #bedifferent #remaininhislove #wearethechurch #restwithgod #godisforus

Sunday, October 13, 2019, New York, NY

321.

> But Jesus said, "That isn't necessary - you feed them."

> Matthew 14:16

The authority God gives us, and His provision.

God has called people in the marketplace to care for those in need. However, let us not look to our abilities or experiences (or our inabilities and inexperiences) to stop us from doing what God may be calling us to. The verses that follow tell of His provision when we accept the call and start moving forward.

Let us not be afraid and trust God for our way forward.

#godprovides #godisable #godisfaithful #gowhengodcalls #nothingisimpossiblewithgod #loveothers #blessothers

Tuesday, October 15, 2019, New York, NY

322.

Their worship is a farce, for they teach man-made ideas as commands from God.'"

Matthew 15:9

Live a good moral life so that you can get to heaven?

Unfortunately, this seems to be the made up concept I hear very often today. When we ask a random stranger in the United States, chances are s/he will say s/he is a Christian. When asked why, they will respond that they live a moral life and is fair in dealing with others. Since s/he is "better" than most people, God of love must accept her/him.

The sad reality, even as shown in this verse, is that many people believe what they want to believe and live in any way they wish thinking they have an argument against God. Yet, none of those people will be accepted by God in the end.

#turntogod #submittogod #feargod #walkwithgod #sovereigngod #wearethechurch #bedifferent

Wednesday, October 16, 2019, New York, NY

323.

"Yes, he does," Peter replied. Then he went into the house. But before he had a chance to speak, Jesus asked him, "What do you think, Peter? Do kings tax their own people or the people they have conquered?" However, we don't want to offend them, so go down to the lake and throw in a line. Open the mouth of the first fish you catch, and you will find a large silver coin. Take it and pay the tax for both of us."

Matthew 17:25, 27

God's providence for His people

1. We will no longer be taxed (burdened, suffer). Jesus already did that for us.

2. During our lives on earth, God will provide for our needs. When we need a coin, it will be provided.

#hisgraceissufficient #godprovides #comeholyspirit #comeasyouare #walkinfaith #weareforgivenandfree

Friday, October 18, 2019, New York, NY

324.

"So those who are last now will be first then, and those who are first will be last."

Matthew 20:16

Work is not everything that produces results. Some of us, especially as we may be wired to think we should be compensated for everything we do, may think we need to do more work (or live better or be kinder to others) to see fruits (such as salvation, acceptance from God, or even a fruitful business). But here, it shows that it is by God's grace that these things happen.

It may even seem unfair that when we have worked so hard and long, to see someone else soar (make more, have more reputation); yet, it is God who allows it. His kindness can lead us to success too, and that is why we should not rely on our worldly thinking or education we may have received.

#sovereigngod #trustgod #turntogod #godisfaithful #bedifferent #letyourlifeshine #walkinfaith

Monday, October 21, 2019, New York, NY

325.

> And asked, "How much will you pay me to betray Jesus to you?" And they gave him thirty pieces of silver. He went on a little farther and bowed with his face to the ground, praying, "My Father! If it is possible, let this cup of suffering be taken away from me. Yet I want your will to be done, not mine."
>
> Matthew 26:15,39

Verse 15. Though this may not be as apparent, there may be times when we turn away from God because of money. One may be when we turn to busy work for the sake of earning more to neglect our relationship with God. Another may be when we take on things that may not be what God had in mind for us because of the greater payout.

How much will you pay to betray Jesus?

In verse 39, it tells us what to do when depressed:

1. Be honest before God. Go to Him intentionally and speak with Him.

2. Ask for His will and trust.

#trustgod #abandonall #remaininhislove #pray #listentogod #turntogod

Sunday, October 27, 2019, New York, NY

326.

He placed it in his own new tomb, which had
been carved out of the rock. Then he rolled a
great stone across the entrance and left.

Matthew 27:60

Things that only businessmen/marketplace professionals are
able to do. Joseph had the resources and land to cover for Jesus' burial.

Remember, each of us have a special calling where God has
placed us.

Take courage, trust, and keep going.

#calling #godprovides #letgoletgod #wehaveallthatweneed #letyourlifeshine #wearethechurch #godhasaplan

Monday, October 28, 2019, New York, NY

Mark

327.

> One day as Jesus was walking along the shore of the Sea of Galilee, he saw Simon and his brother Andrew throwing a net into the water, for they fished for a living. Jesus called out to them, "Come, follow me, and I will show you how to fish for people!"
>
> Mark 1:16-17

We all have our jobs, specialties, businesses, and they are for the purposes of reaching out to others. There is no job that is too big or too small that God cannot use (or make fruitful).

#calling #keepgoing #letyourlifeshine #bethankful #godisforus
Wednesday, October 30, 2019, New York, NY

328.

> Later, Levi invited Jesus and his disciples to his home as dinner guests, along with many tax collectors and other disreputable sinners.
>
> Mark 2:15

We should invite and welcome everyone. We should also go wherever or to whom we are invited. This is how he made God known to them.

This also points to trusting God for who we meet throughout the day. There can be much randomness, or even people we may or may not like but God can use any of those interactions for good.

#sovereigngod #hisgraceissufficient #trustgod #letgoletgod #lookup #letyourlifeshine

Thursday, October 31, 2019, New York, NY

329.

> The seed on the rocky soil represents those who hear the message and immediately receive it with joy. But since they don't have deep roots, they don't last long. They fall away as soon as they have problems or are persecuted for believing God's word. The seed that fell among the thorns represents others who hear God's word, but all too quickly the message is crowded out by the worries of this life, the lure of wealth, and the desire for other things, so no fruit is produced.
>
> Mark 4:16-19

As much as we like the good soil illustration of 30, 60, 100 fold of what was planted, many people fall into rocky or thorny soil. The rocky soil represents those whose hearts are hard and the message cannot take root. They may accept it at first with joy, but it does not last. The thorny soil represents those whose hearts hear the message along with other busyness and complexity of life. The message gets superseded by other priorities and does not go beyond into their work, their families, and into their everyday living. Rather, their faith is temporary, or once-a-Sunday (or even CTO, new term I learned... Christmas and Thanksgiving Only) attenders.

We, as businesspersons for Christ, let us remain in Him (John 15) and not waver in our #1 for our lives.

#makegodpriority #letyourlifeshine #bedifferent #godusesregularpeople #trustgod #gowhengodcalls

Saturday, November 2, 2019, New York, NY

330.

> And he was amazed at their unbelief. Then Jesus
> went from village to village, teaching the people.
> He allowed them to wear sandals but not to take
> a change of clothes. for they still did not
> understand the significance of the miracle of the
> loaves. Their hearts were too hard to take it in.

Mark 6:6,9,52

A chapter on faith.

It begins with how Jesus was shocked/amazed/disappointed with the lack of faith of the people.

Then He tells his followers to be different. He tells them to not do the business-wise thing, which is to go in prepared, but rather to trust God to provide (v.9).

Then the feeding of the 5000. Business-wise thinking would say we need more money and resources, but Jesus says "you feed them." God provides us with what we need. We have more than enough to fulfill his purposes regardless of the circumstances we may "see" in front of us.

#gowhengodcalls #wehaveallthatweneed #breakthrough #trustgod #pray #befruitful #waitongod

Monday, November 4, 2019, New York, NY

331.

> But the disciples had forgotten to bring any
> food. They had only one loaf of bread with them
> in the boat.

Mark 8:14

Do you ever get into a situation that is important but you feel lacking?

Perhaps it is a very important interview for a job of your dreams, or a speech in front of thousands, or anything that may impact your future. You are getting ready for it then you realize, "shoot, I forgot something." Then panic sinks in and you want to quit.

Here, we may be like the disciples that say "we forgot to bring the food" when Jesus has demonstrated that food is not the issue and he can feed people fully if he wants to.

In our times of need, recognize that nothing will ever be perfect (we may miss something, not have something) but God can provide.

It is a question of faith and trust in God. He can, and we depend on Him.

#godisable #trustgod #godisenough #godisfaithful #sovereigngod #wehaveallthatweneed #letgoletgod

Wednesday, November 6, 2019, New York, NY

332.

> Then Elijah and Moses appeared and began talking with Jesus. Then a cloud overshadowed them, and a voice from the cloud said, "This is my dearly loved Son. Listen to him."
>
> Mark 9:4,7

We are not alone.

First thought that came to mind was, how did they know the two men were Elijah and Moses? But one thing that is true about Jesus or even the disciples—they were never alone.

We too are in this together. Stand strong, brothers, in all that God has you involved.

#bethereforoneanother #onefamily #loveothers #remaininhislove #wearethechurch #calling #godisforus

Thursday, November 7, 2019, New York, NY

333.

> 17As Jesus was starting out on his way to
> Jerusalem, a man came running up to him, knelt
> down, and asked, "Good Teacher, what must I do
> to inherit eternal life?"

Mark 10:17 (NLT)

"Good"

This rich man came to Jesus seeking advice. Rich man today may be Bill Gates, Jeff Bezos, and the like. Why would they come to Jesus for help? It is because of some influence Jesus had. We too must be influential so that we may have opportunities to share Christ.

This means to not shrink back in face of a challenge or unknown; but rather trust God and move forward. It also means to keep forming relationships, even with unexpected people.

Now, how can we be influential? The underlying message in this chapter may be that it is through humility that Jesus gained followers. Jesus points to welcoming children and the least being the greatest.

Perhaps the message is that God wants, expects, and wants us to aspire to being people of influence, but we get that by denying ourselves and placing our trust in God alone.

#trustgod #makegodpriority #letyourlifeshine #noreligion #notofthisworld #wearethechurch #meaningfullife

Friday, November 8, 2019, New York, NY

334.

> and he stopped everyone from using the Temple
> as a marketplace.

Mark 11:16

Can this message be alluding to our hearts?

Temple = hearts

Jesus doesn't want our minds to have money as our highest priority.

#feargod #worshipgod #abandonall #letyourlifeshine #bedifferent #meaningfullife #lookup

Saturday, November 9, 2019, New York, NY

335.

> He will take you upstairs to a large room that is
> already set up. That is where you should prepare
> our meal. Keep watch and pray, so that you will
> not give in to temptation. For the spirit is willing,
> but the body is weak."

Mark 14:15,38

1. Gods providence.

    Where would you find, at a moments notice, a place to gather, especially one that has been fully furnished for you?

    In every need, if God intends it, it will be available. Do not look at logic or past experiences, but trust God to open doors.

2. Do not give up.

    Some of us may have immediate worries, even today, that keep on circling your mind. At first, we may ask God to help us, but then get bogged down by the worry. God is able to provide (just like above, just like feeding the 5000).

    Let us not give up on prayer, especially on things that matter most to us. He is faithful to complete what He has begun in us.

#godisenough #expectfromgod #godisforus #walkinfaith #trustgod #godisfaithful #calling #godisable

Tuesday, November 12, 2019, New York, NY

336.

> And then he told them, "Go into all the world and preach the Good News to everyone. Anyone who believes and is baptized will be saved. But anyone who refuses to believe will be condemned. And the disciples went everywhere and preached, and the Lord worked through them, confirming what they said by many miraculous signs.

Mark 16:15,16,20

Interesting finding.

"Go into all the world" is actually same greek tense/word used in Matthew 28.19. Instead of "go," the better translation is "along the way" or "as you are going." The call is not to go blindly and do something, but rather to slow down, and work as you are going to live out our lives and build relationships to make disciples. Once we have a relationship, we can share the Gospel to one another within life-on-life relationships.

Result is still the same, people need to believe in Jesus. As God worked miracles through Jesus' disciples, I hope we will see the miracles personally in our lives and demonstrate them along the way too.

#letyourlifeshine #noreligion #wearethechurch #relationshipsmatter #blessothers #expectfromgod

Thursday, November 14, 2019, New York, NY

Luke

337.

> You will have great joy and gladness, and many
> will rejoice at his birth, for he will be great in the
> eyes of the Lord. He must never touch wine or
> other alcoholic drinks. He will be filled with the
> Holy Spirit, even before his birth. And he will turn
> many Israelites to the Lord their God.

Luke 1:14-16

Countercultural.

Modern concept of success may be money earned or fame given. However, God's views are often very different. When we think of John the Baptist, we often do not associate him as a successful person. Rather, he may be viewed as a person isolated in the desert and a madman telling people to repent. This similar lifestyle may perhaps be seen as a beggar in the subways in today's times.

That was God's better plan! Something that would be a "great joy and gladness," one who is "great in the eyes of the Lord."

Verse 16 says why. John had the influence to turn many people to the Lord.

Let us be thankful for the positions, situations, life God has given us and aim towards leading others to Christ wherever God placed us (whether locational, situational, or even by the influence).

We can see that God is able to use unemployed desert madmen, and He can use us too.

#godhasaplan #gowhengodcalls #walkwithgod #submittogod #trustgod #obeygod #pathsstraight #godisforus

Friday, November 15, 2019, New York, NY

390.

> Everyone was expecting the Messiah to come soon, and they were eager to know whether John might be the Messiah.

Luke 3:15

Seeking a savior from our current situation/circumstances.

People back then, especially the "crowds" (or most people), looked forward to some Messiah. They probably believed that this Messiah will restore their riches, status, and other things they may have wanted or lost.

However, as we know, the Messiah did not come to restore our fortunes. Remember, Jesus was about to be crowned king, but He turned away from that. That is because the heart is what matters, and the riches of eternal life is what He wants us for us.

On earth, God may give us success, even in worldly standards, to make Himself known, as part of a bigger picture story of what He is doing, but He is truly after our hearts and would rather us have an eternal perspective.

#heartmatters #godisfaithful #godhasaplan #godusesregularpeople #sovereigngod #honorgod #makegodpriority

Sunday, November 17, 2019, New York, NY

339.

The crowd was listening to everything Jesus said. And because he was nearing Jerusalem, he told them a story to correct the impression that the Kingdom of God would begin right away. Before he left, he called together ten of his servants and divided among them ten pounds of silver, saying, `Invest this for me while I am gone.' "`Yes,' the king replied, `and to those who use well what they are given, even more will be given. But from those who do nothing, even what little they have will be taken away.

Luke 19:11,13, 26

We are here because God's work in us is not completed yet. He has given us all the abilities, resources, and anything else we may need to complete the mission.

At first, I felt a bit discouraged wondering what if I do not measure up? In this passage, we can see that the "master" was not happy with the person who was given one talent when he just gave back what he had to the "master." Then I realized that the problem was that this person was idle and he did not do anything with what was given to him.

So then, as long as we don't stop (growing, trying, trusting), God will enable us to be fruitful (have meaning in our lives, build for our eternal home).

It is not time yet, and we can produce for the kingdom with what He has given us. Let us not shrink back, let us not give up on the fight. He is more than enough to meet our needs.

#godisenough #gowhengodcalls #keepgoing #hisgraceissufficient #mygodissobig #visionary #noworries

Tuesday, December 3, 2019, New York, NY

340.

"Did John's authority to baptize come from heaven, or was it merely human?"

Luke 20:4

In life, we may do things out of the ordinary—this is what we call leadership and/or taking risks. We can do them without worrying about who authorized us to do so. This also calls us to trust in the Lord in all things—our businesses, our families, our futures and present—so that we can say that we do these things because the Lord has led us to them.

#gowhengodcalls #letyourlifeshine #wehaveallthatweneed #hisgraceissufficient #walkinfaith #calling #letgoletgod

Wednesday, December 4, 2019, New York, NY

341.

For they have given a tiny part of their surplus, but she, poor as she is, has given everything she has."

Luke 21:4

Giving all to Jesus matters.

God gave some people more resources than others to fulfill their unique callings. Do not justify yourself by the amount that you give, as it all belongs to the Lord. What God gives, He can easily take away. Instead, give your all to the Lord. Your family, your business/work, your church, and all your relationships, they all belong to God. It is that heart God is looking for, and He can give you much more than that if it is good for you (because He is good). So trust God and don't hold on to the things of the world.

#abandonall #heartmatters #wehaveallthatweneed #letyourlifeshine #blessingsfromgod

Thursday, June 11, 2020, Old Tappan, NJ USA

342.

> Then Satan entered into Judas Iscariot, who was
> one of the twelve disciples,

Satan is like a virus, he can gain access to a person that is vulnerable from cycles of sin. He just needs a foothold then will continue to use the person in worse and worse ways and make his foothold bigger.

Jesus is like the antivirus. He closes up those holes of vulnerabilities. Satan cannot get a foothold because we are protected.

We need to go to Jesus every day to the protection up to date so we remain in His protection.

#godisourstrength #wehaveallthatweneed #trustgod #listentogod #lovegod #favorwithgod #blessingsfromgod

Friday, June 12, 2020, Old Tappan, NJ USA

343.

> He will take you upstairs to a large room that is
> already set up. That is where you should prepare
> our meal."

Luke 22:12

Businessmen that has much are able to do this. Provide a large room so that people can gather and even prepare a meal for them.

When younger, I thought Jesus was doing some mind tricks (Jedi stuff) to cause some random person to provide a place for them. I think Jesus had pre-coordinated with someone who had a spare guest room.

As businessmen, we tend to have inventory of things such as our products, locations/meeting spaces, or simply money and resources. We have the ability to supply these to the Church or those in need. We can also pray asking God to fill us so that we may, through our businesses, do that.

May we all be great influential leaders in the world to make God known.

#blessothers #givetoothers #bemerciful #godprovides #calling #wehaveallthatweneed #expectfromgod

Friday, December 6, 2019, New York, NY

344.

Now there was a good and righteous man named Joseph. He was a member of the Jewish high council, but he had not agreed with the decision and actions of the other religious leaders. He was from the town of Arimathea in Judea, and he was waiting for the Kingdom of God to come.

Luke 23:50-51

Living with knowledge that God is here.

Luke describes that Joseph (a Jew) "was waiting for the Kingdom of God to come" and held thoughts that were different from other Jewish people. Majority of the Jewish people stopped believing in the power of God and just lived on perhaps focusing on the execution of keeping their moral living.

Can we say the same about Christians? Do we just focus on living a good moral life but not believe in the power of God?

Let us be open to hear God to direct us in our families, businesses, church, and even our small group because we know that when He acts, it's always much greater than we can imagine or think. Let us too wait for the Kingdom of God to come with a longing expectation.

#comeholyspirit #renewal #walkinfaith #meaningfullife #lookup #favorwithgod #waitongod #expectfromgod

Saturday, December 7, 2019, New York, NY

345.

> But the story sounded like nonsense to the men, so they did not believe it. However, Peter jumped up and ran to the tomb to look. Stooping, he peered in and saw the empty linen wrappings; then he went home again, wondering what had happened.
>
> Luke 24:11-12

Nonsense to the world may be to where God calls us.

The world relies on what we see, and makes sense in the physical world. For Christians, we believe in faith that we ought to take action even in the things that do not make sense.

Let us not be dependent on the physical world, but trust God even when things may sound like "nonsense." Peter took immediate action because he was familiar with how God did things when it seemed like nonsense to others. Let it be familiar to us as well.

#walkwithgod #bedifferent #listentogod #befruitful #trustgod #gowhengodcalls #walkinfaith

Sunday, June 14, 2020, Ridgefield, NJ USA

346.

> Then the two from Emmaus told their story of
> how Jesus had appeared to them as they were
> walking along the road, and how they had
> recognized him as he was breaking the bread.

Luke 24:35

Power of eating together.

When we meet through the rush of life then go straight into other agendas, we may not be able to settle, observe our surroundings, and even "get the message."

Here, eating together enabled the two to settle and see (recognize Jesus).

This is for us, in our gatherings, and also for the Sabbath rest today.

Have a relaxed, wonderful time with God today. May you "recognize" Him throughout the day.

#restwithgod #bethereforoneanother #walkwithgod #listentogod #waitongod #godprovides

Sunday, December 8, 2019, New York, NY

John

347.

> Though his ministry follows mine, I'm not even worthy to be his slave and untie the straps of his sandal."

John 1:27

Our call may be to support others.

The education that we received tells us that we must be successful and that we must do whatever it takes for that purpose.

However, in God's economy, in His purposes in our lives, we may be called to rather serve others. When we are faced with opportunities to advance over others, or an opportunity to help, lets pause and ask God before moving forward. Who knows if our service to another is what changes the world?

#trustgod #listentogod #heartmatters #letgoletgod #pray #honorgod #letmywordsbefew #godhasaplan

Tuesday, December 10, 2019, New York, NY

348.

> I did not recognize him as the Messiah, but I have been baptizing with water so that he might be revealed to Israel."

John 1:31

Things Only God Can Do.

John 1 sets the stage for the ministries of Jesus. Before Jesus began, there was a man named John, who is better known as "John the Baptist." He knew he had a God-given mission and was faithful to keep to it. In verse 23, it says "John replied in the words of Isaiah the prophet, 'I am the voice of one calling in the desert, "Make straight the way for the Lord."'" However, even though he was given this "high" position, an awesome mission in the eyes of many, he did not take his high stature to act as if He was God.

This is the trap people of high positions or titles often fall into. Only God is able to heal and only God is able to save, and only God should receive all the glory. However, when sometimes, even in our ministries, we recognize that we may know the Bible well, we gain titles, and we begin to serve in various parts of ministries (lead Bible studies, take part in the worship team, etc), we may begin to think and act as if "we are God."

Do you ever recall yourself saying, because I'm so musically talented, my presence in the praise team will make things well? I know how the church ought to be run and so, under my direction, everything will be good? God uses me (or has used me) in a mighty way that when I pray for a certain person, s/he would be healed or would feel better? It is true that God uses people (us!) for His purposes; however, just like John, we should never forget that there are things only God can do. It is not about us; it is about Him. We should not take the glory that He deserves even when He uses us.

Only God can bring about salvation. Only He can bring about healing from people's deepest pains. Only He can deliver us from our financial situations. Only He can put peace in our hearts. Only He can show us His deep love for us. It's not about us, but about Him. We don't do anything, He does! We just see and listen to simply join in on what He is doing.

As people who love God and are willing to be molded by Him, God will show us many amazing things in and through our lives, and when He does, let us not become arrogant. Rather, let us push the glory back to Him "that he might be revealed to Israel" (v. 31). These are things only God can do—not us.

#godisourstrength #listentogod #blessingsfromgod #blessothers #walkwithgod #godisfaithful #godprovides

Sunday, January 24, 2010, New York, NY

349.

> The next day Jesus decided to go to Galilee. He found Philip and said to him, "Come, follow me." Philip was from Bethsaida, Andrew and Peter's hometown. Philip went to look for Nathanael and told him, "We have found the very person Moses and the prophets wrote about! His name is Jesus, the son of Joseph from Nazareth." "Nazareth!" exclaimed Nathanael. "Can anything good come from Nazareth?" "Come and see for yourself," Philip replied. As they approached, Jesus said, "Now here is a genuine son of Israel— a man of complete integrity." "How do you know about me?" Nathanael asked Jesus replied, "I could see you under the fig tree before Philip found you."
>
> John 1:43-48

Nathaniel may seem like a proud person, or perhaps he only experienced not-so-good from people who have come from Nazareth. But Jesus happens to come from there.

It shows that God uses the humble and unexpected things and makes good of them. God uses the humble people, not the people who are so sure of themselves.

#heartmatters #letgoletgod #befruitful #letyourlifeshine #abandonall #bedifferent #meaningfullife #visionary

Saturday, May 28, 2011, Leonia, NJ USA

350.

The wine supply ran out during the festivities, so Jesus' mother told him, "They have no more wine."

John 2:3

We never lack. God fills us with the best things. Simply trust, lean not on your own understanding, acknowledge Him in all your ways (See Proverbs 3:5-6).

#godisenough #wehaveallthatweneed #hisgraceissufficient #godisable #godprovides #trustgod #breakthrough

Wednesday, December 11, 2019, New York, NY

> In the Temple area he saw merchants selling
> cattle, sheep, and doves for sacrifices; he also
> saw dealers at tables exchanging foreign money.
> Jesus made a whip from some ropes and chased
> them all out of the Temple. He drove out the
> sheep and cattle, scattered the money changers'
> coins over the floor, and turned over their tables.
> Then, going over to the people who sold doves,
> he told them, "Get these things out of here. Stop
> turning my Father's house into a marketplace!"

John 2:14-16

Business Relationships with God.

Do you ever find yourself trying to make deals with God? In our business-minded society, we learn that this is normal to try to negotiate what seems best to us.

Even in our friend, college, or even church relationships, we often seek what benefits us from the relationship. Maybe we need to learn to accept people as they are and love them despite their flaws. In our modern day, fast-paced lifestyle and broken families show us that relationships are not considered important to many people. In fact, as a result of this, many people, perhaps even us, don't know how to hold and nurture our relationships.

Isn't this another reason why divorce rates are so high? Married people have not learned to build relationships, but rather to go through the motions of emotions/love. When that fades, there's no foundation of relationship to lean on. And of course, they don't see the problem within themselves and rather blame the other person. Then life goes on as if nothing happened; because we all have things to do, careers to pursue, and money to make.

Apparently, relationships are not as important as our personal goals and success. We need to admit that there are many times we want to somehow manipulate God just as we want to manipulate our relationships.

If you're a guy, and you just want to win a girl's heart (perhaps out of love/emotion), we may perform a series of events to obtain what we want. We may be seeking to find a way to do that with God. Perhaps you may perform a study of Scriptures *just enough* to "make" God give you what you want. How many of you have said, "I prayed about something and nothing happened, and therefore, God must not be real." or "He must not love me." This is why it's so hard for even Christians nowadays to experience God—to know His love for us and His mighty power that is at work within and through us.

Christianity has become such a weak, wimpy religion, one where anyone can join nominally (80% of US claims to be a Christian today), but has no power, no difference than from those who do not believe. Divorce rates for Christians are no different than those who claim to not be Christians!

People who claim to be Christians are often sad and depressed even though Scriptures talk about "joy divine." To the world, it may seem as if Christianity is dead, and if so, why would it interest them?

I want to share a new concept with you, if you haven't heard me talk about it—Christianity is not the religion for which Jesus came (<— I've been thinking of writing a book with this title). It's about a relationship.

With your mother or father, you would not manipulate the situation to force the parent to give in to you. Maybe since many of us are older, we may be able to pull tricks over our parents, but try to think of yourself as a little kid (like my son's age, 3 years old) and trying to pull a fast one on an adult. God doesn't want that, and of course He sees right through our hearts.

God doesn't want a business relationship with us. He wants a father-son (mother-child) relationship—where it's all out of pure love for each other where both find satisfaction.

Developing our relationship with God is how we can see the things God is doing and we can join in with Him to see and demonstrate to others His power. As we join and partner with God, we may find that God blesses us in our regular lives (see Matthew 6:33-34).

As we put all our trust in God, we can find our lives to be without worries, and therefore, joyful because we know God is in control! We have hope that He will turn all the bad for good.

So, I encourage you, develop a relationship with God. (If you're not sure how—all you have to do is let me know and I'll walk with you through it).

Couple of things for all of us to reflect on:

1. How are your people relationship skills? Do you find yourself lacking it? Let me or someone you believe can help you know, and work on it.

If you learn to build relationships with other people, you may better recognize how God wants to have a relationship with you. You will learn that it is not about what you "do," or how you "try to do" things that causes him to reward you. He wants to give and He loves simply because you are His child. We just need to learn to accept His love and grace just as He gives it to us, and relate with Him.

2. Do you find yourself trying to make deals with God? Do you ever say, "God, if you would give me XYZ, I would do whatever for you"—that's not going to work. God sees through your "business" plans. He wants to have a relationship with you instead.

3. If you have been a Christian for a while, and believe in all the things in the Bible, but don't see His power or guidance in your life—try to think about why. It may be because you consider God to be someone who is far away to just deal with your problems and issues. You may not consider Him like a Father with whom you ought to relate to, converse with, and rely on in all of life's matters. He's seeking you to surrender all of you to Him. What are you holding back? What skills / talents / abilities do you find yourself relying on as your own strength? Maybe you need to stop making deals with God as if you have something of value that you can negotiate with God for a reward. He wants to relate with you. Instead of doing business deals with God, but let's walk with Him.

#walkwithgod #pathsstraight #godlovesus #godusesregularpeople #godisforus #lifetransformation #abandonall

Tuesday, January 26, 2010, New York, NY

352.

Because of the miraculous signs Jesus did in Jerusalem at the Passover celebration, many began to trust in him. But Jesus did not trust them, because he knew human nature. No one needed to tell him what mankind is really like.

John 2:23-25

Faith of people are fickle. They say they believe in Jesus, then turn back as circumstances change. That's why as believers, we must keep growing in faith, or grow in having constant, unshakable faith. Not growing may lead to shrinking back in faith, or becoming no different than the rest of the world.

#bedifferent #makegodpriority #wearethechurch #remaininhislove #hisgraceissufficient #godisfaithful

Tuesday, June 16, 2020, Old Tappan, NJ USA

353.

"The wind blows wherever it wants. Just as you can hear the wind but cannot tell where it comes from or where it is going, so you cannot explain how people are born of the Spirit." Jesus replied, "You are a respected Jewish teacher, and yet you don't understand these things?

John 3:8,10

"You cannot explain … and you don't understand?"

When we have some knowledge (we understand something), should not we also be able to teach it? But Jesus says to a highly prestigious teacher that rebirth cannot be explained, but he should be able to know it, understand it, and believe it.

That is the case for faith. This also means that we do not need to worry about what we need to say for evangelism or anything else in life. For some things may not be explainable; yet, when God wills, the listeners will be able to understand. It is not dependent on us. God is in control.

#sovereigngod #godprovides #gowhengodcalls #listentogod #expectfromgod #trustgod #visionary #calling

Thursday, December 12, 2019, New York, NY

354.

He had to go through Samaria on the way.

John 4:4

In life, we too may need to go through places, especially through where other people are, that many people would normally avoid.

Instead of hurrying through it, Jesus went through it restfully. Let us too not rush but be dependent on the Father's leading. He may have a purpose for you as you go.

The same is true in our work and in all that we do. Be available for God to interject and speak to us.

#listentogod #beavailable #comeholyspirit #pathsstraight #abandonall #heartmatters #letgoletgod #trustgod

Thursday, June 18, 2020, Old Tappan, NJ USA

355.

> "I cannot, sir," the sick man said, "for I have no one to put me into the pool when the water bubbles up. Someone else always gets there ahead of me."

John 5:7

Seeing beyond the person's needs.

The lame man just wanted to jump into the water, as if he forgot that he actually just wanted to be healed. Two points:

1. For us, let us not be blinded by the tasks ahead of us, but continue to go after the greater calling God has given to us.

2. As we see others, let us not just look at their next step, but even beyond to enable them, pray for them, guide them to God's greater calling for their lives. This man may have forgotten why he wanted to jump into the pool in the first place, and maybe Jesus wants to restore the original purpose he had so that he may follow God with all his heart.

#visionary #turntogod #listentogod #comeholyspirit #beavailable #bemerciful #remaininhislove #calling

Saturday, December 14, 2019, New York, NY

"You search the Scriptures because you think
they give you eternal life. But the Scriptures
point to me! Yet you refuse to come to me to
receive this life.

John 5:39-40

Let's try rephrasing these verses in our modern day terms. "You diligently go to church because by attending, you feel you are spiritual, completing the righteous duty of a believer, meeting God's command about the sabbath, and because Sang is cool (<—yeah, I added this part!).

But seriously, it is sad that many people go to church for years, some for decades, and some, until they die *without really knowing God.* Yes, people who attend church regularly may end up in hell and they may never receive the blessings God has for them.

How do you view church? Is it an organization you attend just for the sake of doing it? If so, you are wasting your time.

For some of you who are "trying" the church thing out ~ I encourage you to at least go all the way for the short duration you plan to attend, and strive to meet and experience God instead of just standing at the side lines. What is the point of your wasting your time coming and leaving while not knowing whether God is real or not? Would you stay for a decade or more just as many people do and never find out how much God loves you personally? How God speaks to you? And how God cares about the pains and sorrows in your life?

If you're not interested in meeting and experiencing God, what's the point? Why bother? So when the pastor ever directs you to pray, I encourage you to go deep in prayer and tell God all that is in your heart.

And to many of you who are seeking, ask God to reveal Himself to you. Ask God to help you through your tough situation in life. And when the pastor tells you to sing, sing with all your heart, give it all you got with the heart intent that you want to meet and experience God.

He will talk to you, and give you the guidance on what you ought to do and where to go from where you are. (If you need help with this, just let me know).

For some of you churchy people, check your heart that you are not working the Scriptures and your involvement in church to manipulate God.

There are many, even pastors, who study Scriptures and make a whole course or a formula on how to make God work for us. Some pastors actually become pastors because they believe this position would give them this "special privilege" where they may either manipulate God or manipulate people who may see them as ones God speaks to in a special voice. Be careful!

Even though studies and going deep into Scripture is beneficial, and though becoming stewards of God is an awesome calling, we must recognize that God cannot be manipulated, for He is God!

Scripture is for us to understand His heart—His desire to build a relationship with us. You don't need a seminary degree to know God or hear from God. You don't need to be a pastor's pet to have a deep relationship with God. God gave all of us the innate value—His children—that allows us to connect with Him.

That's the missing part in many of our lives, a relationship with our Creator, our Maker, our heavenly Father. So, don't do the church thing—but rather, come to meet with God and form a relationship with Him.

This is the reason for which Jesus came—to love us, that we may love Him back.

#godlovesus #lovegod #turntogod #trustgod #bethankful #renewal #breakthrough #heartmatters #letgoletgod

Thursday, January 28, 2010, New York, NY

A huge crowd kept following him wherever he went, because they saw his miraculous signs as he healed the sick. "Tell everyone to sit down," Jesus said. So they all sat down on the grassy slopes. Jesus replied, "I tell you the truth, you want to be with me because I fed you, not because you understood the miraculous signs. But don't be so concerned about perishable things like food. Spend your energy seeking the eternal life that the Son of Man can give you. For God the Father has given me the seal of his approval." Many of his disciples said, "This is very hard to understand. How can anyone accept it?" Jesus was aware that his disciples were complaining, so he said to them, "Does this offend you? At this point many of his disciples turned away and deserted him.

John 6:2,10,26-27,60-61,66

Jesus is not after the crowd, but the few.

If Jesus was leading a church as a pastor, there would not be a lot of people—because only a few people would remain. I bet He would attract the crowds, but only some would be faithful.

Some people come to church for personal reasons such as for personal spirituality, as a duty, to make business connections, and to be amongst friends. Yet, as Jesus did, the church (that's us!) ought to reach people meeting their personal needs. Jesus demonstrated this as He healed sicknesses, dealt with problems people had, and even feeding the 5000 men that followed him. However, that was not the end-goal for Jesus.

He first reached for them so that they may reach for God back. You see, Jesus could have built a bigger crowd—heck, he could've even been king (see verse 15); but that's not what He wanted—He did not want a crowd, He wanted the few.

When the crowd gathered, Jesus gave a message that challenged all those people who followed him (see verses 25-59). He said, "I am the bread of life. He who comes to me will never go hungry, and he who believes in me will never be thirsty" (v. 35). People had hard time accepting Jesus as the way to God. No, their hearts were not after God, but instead, they wanted Jesus to deal with more of their problems, feed their hunger, and see more signs that can benefit THEM. They did not care about a relationship with nor even knowing God. They were focused on their own needs and desires.

Jesus basically said, that's not the reason for which I came. I want you to know God—and you can do that only by accepting me, the Bread of Life. He is the food that never spoils, the One who can provide for all our needs.

This required faith, and it was not a straight up logic that people could accept. How could believing and trusting in someone take care of all of my problems and pains? People then were smart just like us. They could tell this was not a logical process.

Then many walked away. They wanted more proof of how God can benefit their lives, and Jesus wasn't giving any. You see, Jesus was never after the crowd. He was never after complacent people who may join bigger churches because they can just go in and come out. Jesus was after the few that would believe in Him and would form a relationship with God.

Are you one of the crowd? The other kind of crowd is also evident, people who are constantly seeking for proof of His existence, even though God has touched and revealed Himself to them, then saying God is not real—then walking away. For those of you that are seeking right now, I encourage you to ask God to reveal Himself to you and when you receive the response, stop challenging God for more proof or benefit in your life; instead, now, you should believe and follow.

Are you the crowd, or the few?

Applications:

1. How does Jesus relate to your everyday life?

2. When you study your patterns of prayers, do you tend to just ask for "your" requests? Do you find your attitude to be similar to that of the crowd that Jesus dismissed?

3. If you are a church leader, do you find yourself constantly trying to please the crowd? or are you truly giving the message from Scriptures? Are you challenging, and even offending some of the members?

4. I know many of us are intellectuals… yes, in the US, many of us had education and logic is highly favored. Yet, faith is not something that can be proved by science or fact (see Hebrews 11:1). Do you believe in God who cannot be proven? Do you believe in Jesus even through the hard times when it feels like the desert? Do you believe in the heavenly Father even though life at home (with family) hurts you? (see v. 26-27)

Be the Few.

#letyourlifeshine #walkinfaith #letgoletgod #pathsstraight #comeholyspirit #godisfaithful #relationshipsmatter

Friday, January 29, 2010, New York, NY

358.

> When Jesus saw that they were ready to force him to be their king, he slipped away into the hills by himself.
>
> John 6:15

Do not be who others want you to be or whom the world aspires to be great.

Unless God calls you to them, do not set your heart to be like an executive or a director. This verse shows Jesus in a strange light. He was about to be crowned king, the highest prestige one may have (or is it?).

Jesus knew His calling and purpose and was not swayed by other "temptations."

Same for us, let us know our callings and do not let other things get in the way, including temptations (other opportunities that may lead us astray), lust, and other distractions. We have a great calling, a great destiny. Let us remain close to God and fulfill it during our lives.

#letyourlifeshine #bedifferent #wearethechurch #meaningfullife #narrowpath #mygodissobig #lifetransformation

Sunday, December 15, 2019, New York, NY

359.

> And Jesus' brothers said to him, "Leave here and go to Judea, where your followers can see your miracles! You cannot become famous if you hide like this! If you can do such wonderful things, show yourself to the world!" For even his brothers did not believe in him. Jesus replied, "Now is not the right time for me to go, but you can go anytime. Those who speak for themselves want glory only for themselves, but a person who seeks to honor the one who sent him speaks truth, not lies. Look beneath the surface so you can judge correctly."
>
> John 7:3-6, 18, 24

Whether for ourselves or our businesses.

Its ok when we do not go after the recognition. It may not be the time, or it may not be what God wants you to do. Do not worry about what happens, or even opportunities lost. God is in control of the results and He cares for you. Trust God with your circumstances and He will guide us in the best ways.

#trustgod #gowhengodcalls #godisfaithful #godprovides #restwithgod #listentogod #comeholyspirit

Monday, December 16, 2019, New York, NY

360.

> You cannot become famous if you hide like this!
> If you can do such wonderful things, show
> yourself to the world!" For even his brothers did
> not believe in him.

People who do not fear God and rely on business strategies such as marketers may tell you to aim to go public. However, we need to hear from God. The brothers and sisters who love us too must hear from God and share what the Lord says.

As Christians, we do not rely on what the world teaches, but how God directs us, which may be through our relationships.

#bethereforoneanother #onefamily #loveothers #blessothers #godprovides #godisfaithful #comeholyspirit

Sunday, June 21, 2020, Orangeburg, NY USA

361.

> But early the next morning he was back again at
> the Temple. A crowd soon gathered, and he sat
> down and taught them.

John 8:2

Teaching in world of confusion.

Back in Jesus' days, I imagine many were either unschooled or learned, and so, only a few people in the temple would get up to speak what is in their mind while others listened. Since there were probably no other place to gain education, if someone has some "knowledge," they would be willing to listen and "learn."

We live in days where knowledge is everywhere: on the web and on our phones. In these times, 1) let us be influential and ready to teach so that we are ready when we are given an opportunity to share with someone who wishes to learn. 2) Especially these days, true learning occurs through relationships or small groups. Let us demonstrate the love of God through our actions so that others may learn.

#letyourlifeshine #calling #renewal #pathsstraight #comeholyspirit #bedifferent #visionary #blessothers

Tuesday, December 17, 2019, New York, NY

362.

> As Jesus was walking along, he saw a man who had been blind from birth.
>
> John 9:1

On the way, as we are walking along, as we live on.

These are terms where we do not restrict time, as some of us may do on Lord's Days at church. These are terms where we have expectation for God to do amazing things as we recognize that God can show up at any time, interjecting whatever we may be doing, and direct us or do His thing.

Note that in Matthew 28, the Great Commission says, make disciples along the way. Treasure the brotherhood even when it may feel like things are slow or nothing is happening.

#godisfaithful #comeholyspirit #makegodpriority #abandonall #befruitful #bedifferent #walkinfaith

Wednesday, December 18, 2019, New York, NY

363.

> Then Jesus told him, "I entered this world to render judgment—to give sight to the blind and to show those who think they see that they are blind." "If you were blind, you wouldn't be guilty," Jesus replied. "But you remain guilty because you claim you can see."
>
> John 9:39,41

As much as we want to pass by this verse assuming it is talking about people who may not know God—or people certainly not like us—this message was given to the Pharisees, the people who thought they believed in God the most.

We can see how frail we are by the times we get angry at others or by things that occupy our minds. It is human nature to think we are more capable than we really are. Instead, these verses call us to recognize that we are guilty and that we are blind so that we may truly see. In this verse, it is about sight, but it is for all things beyond that.

Let us go to Jesus like this man who has been healed and say, "Lord I want to believe."

#comeholyspirit #expectfromgod #turntogod #renewal #breakthrough #hisgraceissufficient #godisfaithful

Tuesday, June 23, 2020, Northvale, NJ USA

364.

> No one can take my life from me. I sacrifice it voluntarily. For I have the authority to lay it down when I want to and also to take it up again. For this is what my Father has commanded."
>
> John 10:18

Our free will to give up so that we may serve others.

Just as Jesus can lay it down and pick it up again, there are times when we may free up our resources (time, money, and effort) for others then take the lead as needed.

Servanthood, or followership, is a leadership tool, and something God calls us to as well.

#letyourlifeshine #bedifferent #wehaveallthatweneed #submittogod #abandonall #calling #letgoletgod

Thursday, December 19, 2019, New York, NY

365.

> Jesus replied, "I have already told you, and you don't believe me. The proof is the work I do in my Father's name. Jesus said, "At my Father's direction I have done many good works. For which one are you going to stone me?" Don't believe me unless I carry out my Father's work. But if I do his work, believe in the evidence of the miraculous works I have done, even if you don't believe me. Then you will know and understand that the Father is in me, and I am in the Father."
>
> John 10:25,32,37-38

As we seek to be like Jesus, it may cause us to think we need to do "work" like Jesus did. Here, the translation for "work" is actually "doing." The passage can be read this way, "Why don't you believe that God is working through me? The proof is the doing that I do in my Father's Name. At my Father's direction, I have been doing good."

Jesus is simply doing as God guides Him. It does not equate to us accomplishing or showing results of what we perceive as the reason for the "work," but rather it is simply hearing from God and doing it. This is repeated in verse 37, where He says to believe as long as He is doing the work of the Father.

To be like Jesus, we too must hear the voice of the Father and do His work (results are up to him, and that is not our concern). He will take care of all our needs as we do as the Father guides us (see also Matthew 6:33). Others can come to believe as we do the Father's will.

#listentogod #calling #bedifferent #beavailable #rightwithgod #waitongod #trustgod #submittogod #blessothers

Wednesday, June 24, 2020, Closter, NJ USA

366.

> For it was because of him that many of the people had deserted them and believed in Jesus. But despite all the miraculous signs Jesus had done, most of the people still did not believe in him.
>
> John 12:11,37

Do not be focused on the count (quantity), but rather, the impacts for individuals (quality).

Here, the Pharisees, the church leaders in our context, was upset because some guy named Jesus was pulling people out of their "church." Jesus did not think in numbers, gathering the masses, but rather, in caring for the person: bringing healing, teaching them the right thing, etc.

We too, in our churches, or even in our small groups, let us care for one another deeply, the impact that occurs over time, and not consider the results by the numbers.

Verse 37 also shows us something interesting. In the view of the Pharisees, Jesus was pulling people out, but in reality, "most" of the people still did not believe. Here:

1. Jesus was focused on those who did not believe in Jesus, not just the Christians, and we should too!

2. Pharisees were thinking small, or focusing on "maintaining" their members. Today's churches tend to be this way too. As businessmen for Christ, we have the world in front of us. We can impact many people. Let us not forget that and think bigger, as our God is a big, great, nothing-is-impossible God.

#mygodissobig #nothingisimpossiblewithgod #wehaveallthatweneed #hisgraceissufficient #visionary #calling

Saturday, December 21, 2019, New York, NY

367.

> So now I am giving you a new commandment: Love each other. Just as I have loved you, you should love each other. Your love for one another will prove to the world that you are my disciples." Simon Peter asked, "Lord, where are you going?" And Jesus replied, "You cannot go with me now, but you will follow me later." "But why cannot I come now, Lord?" he asked. "I'm ready to die for you." Jesus answered, "Die for me? I tell you the truth, Peter-before the rooster crows tomorrow morning, you will deny three times that you even know me.
>
> John 13:34-38

God is readying me.

When things do not seem to be working out and when we feel as if we are not being fruitful, consider Simon Peter who wanted to go all out and even die for Jesus. Yet, it was not his time, not in God's planning, and so…

I may not be able to follow now, but will follow later. It is not God's timing yet, as God needs to prepare me. God needs to work in me before I can follow.

Trust God. He who started a good work will be faithful to finish it.

#turntogod #trustgod #letgoletgod #walkinfaith #noworries #remaininhislove #letmywordsbefew

Saturday, February 5, 2011, Leonia, NJ USA

368.

> But I will do what the Father requires of me, so that the world will know that I love the Father. Come, let's be going.
>
> John 14:31

But I will do what the Father requires of me.

This can be trials, times of waiting, acts of personal discipline, or pursuits that are against the flesh.

This is what it means to be missional, or a person whose focus is on the mission.

#visionary #trustgod #letgoletgod #submittogod #expectfromgod #godisforus #godisable #beavailable

Sunday, June 28, 2020, Old Tappan, NJ USA

369.

> But in fact, it is best for you that I go away,
> because if I don't, the Advocate won't come. If I
> do go away, then I will send him to you. When
> the Spirit of truth comes, he will guide you into
> all truth. He will not speak on his own but will tell
> you what he has heard. He will tell you about the
> future. He will bring me glory by telling you
> whatever he receives from me. At that time you
> won't need to ask me for anything. I tell you the
> truth, you will ask the Father directly, and he will
> grant your request because you use my name.
> You haven't done this before. Ask, using my
> name, and you will receive, and you will have
> abundant joy.

John 16:7,13,14,23,24

Merry Christmas everyone!

In today's Scripture, Jesus tells us the reason why He came, the reason for Christmas: it is to be with us.

He died so that He may first handle the sin issue, so that He may now dwell among us, walk with us, and personally guide us (v. 13-14).

Regarding anything we may need, when we love God and trust Him, and as a result, we ask for it in Jesus' Name, He will provide (v. 23,24).

Let us celebrate this wonderful news today with a great cheer. Let us ask in His Name anything we need and rest on Him today. Merry Christmas everyone!

#restwithgod #godisenough #wehaveallthatweneed #noworries #godlovesus #comeholyspirit #blessingsfromgod

Wednesday, December 25, 2019, New York, NY

He called out, "Fellows, have you caught any fish?" "No," they replied. Then he said, "Throw out your net on the right-hand side of the boat, and you'll get some!" So they did, and they couldn't haul in the net because there were so many fish in it. "Bring some of the fish you've just caught," Jesus said.

John 21:5,6,10

For 2020, let us rely on God for all providence.

After college, when I signed up and got accepted to officer training in the USAF, I got my first taste in how a company (or government) can cover me when I am working for them. When we think about progressing in our businesses, or even our lives, we may think "how do I handle X, then Y, then ABC?"

The Air Force had set up my flights, lodging, and everything else in between to get me to my destination and settle in the new places. This is to say, we may not have everything together, and we may not even know what we need, but we have a Father who loves us and is in complete control over all that we see (and do not!). And He's got it covered.

Let us not worry about tomorrow, but be thankful and trust Him for the systems of provisions (Everything! Not one or two things we may think we may need, but everything.).

Do not fear when your next business/life activities become uncertain, but rather trust God.

We can see in today's passage that

1. Jesus gave the greatest catch, especially when the fishermen, the experts in what they do, could not catch anything. We too may be discouraged in the things we thought we did well in when results are not produced, but God can turn that around!

2. Jesus wants to dine with us, and He provides the package of providing the profits (fish) and even the meal (fish again) and the means (fire by the shore).

We do not need to have prerequisites. He can provide the system for us from where we are. In 2020, let us make God our trust.

#sovereigngod #trustgod #letgoletgod #pathsstraight #wehaveallthatweneed #breakthrough #letyourlifeshine

Monday, December 30, 2019, New York, NY

371.

> After breakfast Jesus asked Simon Peter, "Simon son of John, do you love me more than these?" "Yes, Lord," Peter replied, "you know I love you." "Then feed my lambs," Jesus told him. Jesus repeated the question: "Simon son of John, do you love me?" "Yes, Lord," Peter said, "you know I love you." "Then take care of my sheep," Jesus said. A third time he asked him, "Simon son of John, do you love me?" Peter was hurt that Jesus asked the question a third time. He said, "Lord, you know everything. You know that I love you." Jesus said, "Then feed my sheep.
>
> John 21:15-17

Complete Forgiveness.

How many of you feel like a failure? as if you don't measure up?

Some of you may be struggling with your failures before God— how you've failed Him so many times that you feel worthless, and as if God could never accept you again.

I want to share with you the grace that we have received. God knew that we can never make it on our own. He knew we would fail in our own strength. He knew we needed someone who would take the place of our failures. We all know who that is.

More importantly, let us remember our rightful place. We are the children of God, not a servant or a nobody, but a heir to what God has for us. We have lost this sonship (daughtership) because of sin. Now, see what Jesus does...

The story above (John 21:15-17) links with John 18:15-27, where Peter denied Jesus three times—three failures. Jesus forgives Peter's sin completely by iterating through this forgiveness process three times. With the complete forgiveness, Peter is restored and reinstated to his rightful position with God.

The following verses (18-19) talk about the original plan God had for Peter (if you look at the beginning verses, try verse 3, Peter had gone back to his old job of fishing, which was not what God had in mind for Peter). It was through this reinstatement that Peter's relationship with God was restored. This restoration could have only occurred through complete forgiveness of sins, which only Jesus can do.

From here on, Peter was able to live to his fullest, which is not be a fisherman all his life, but do amazing things through his life by following God's will for him.

So, today and tomorrow – it is a chance for us to put all our failures out to Jesus and receive His complete forgiveness. (Of course, I can walk you through this at another time, but it's these times of "revivals" where you can really feel refreshed and re-secure a relationship with God). I encourage you to try to come if at all possible.

Couple of things to think about:

1. Do you know where you are going in life? What you will do in ten years, twenty years? I encourage you to not remain a fisherman, but find out what God has in plan for you. It begins with His forgiveness, which leads to your reinstatement with your relationship with God.

2. Do you feel worthless, as if you can never measure up to the world's standards? You're never good enough, not pretty enough, not educated enough, not skilled enough? First, recognize that the world is after useless things—so don't compare yourself with others—we know we have a greater calling! Second, bring all your failures to Jesus, he can reconcile your weaknesses, and God will direct your steps. You are a child of God, one who is forgiven and reinstated as God's child.

372.

> Peter's words pierced their hearts, and they said to him and to the other apostles, "Brothers, what should we do?"

Acts 2:37

Gents, I want to share something about the importance of what we are doing as we gather together and encourage one another.

Here, the men gathered together, and God spoke through one of them (Peter). The brothers looked to each other and discussed their next actions as a result of their acceptance that God has spoken to them through Peter. Then they changed the world.

Let us not grow weary of meeting together and never cease to remember and hold the expectation that God is doing something great through each of us. Do not ever think that our meetings are in vain or may be a waste of time.

Remember, by the Pentecost, people were uncertain of what is to come. Yet, God came, spoke to them, and they were sent out. They changed the world.

#godusesregularpeople #comeholyspirit #mygodissobig #calling #wehaveallthatweneed #hisgraceissufficient

Friday, July 19, 2019, New York, NY

Romans

<No Entries Here>

1Corinthians

<No Entries Here>

2Corinthians

<No Entries Here>

Galatians

373.

> Those who are trying to force you to be
> circumcised want to look good to others. They
> don't want to be persecuted for teaching that
> the cross of Christ alone can save.

Galatians 6:12

People who claim we need to live righteous lives—in the eyes of the people—are people who believe the law. They may be people who are proud of their heritage, education, experiences, careers, and positions but we ought to humble ourselves and seek Christ.

Following Christ is for the broken, the rejected, the hurting, and the suffering. The Gospel asks nothing more than for us to believe and put our faith in God.

#bedifferent #notofthisworld #comeholyspirit #bethankful #letmywordsbefew #meaningfullife #abandonall

Saturday, February 12, 2011, Nyack, NY

Ephesians

374.

> I also pray that you will understand the incredible greatness of God's power for us who believe him. This is the same mighty power that raised Christ from the dead and seated him in the place of honor at God's right hand in the heavenly realms. Now he is far above any ruler or authority or power or leader or anything else—not only in this world but also in the world to come. God has put all things under the authority of Christ and has made him head over all things for the benefit of the church. And the church is his body; it is made full and complete by Christ, who fills all things everywhere with himself.

Ephesians 1:19-23

How often we forget.

As we go through the struggles of the day, frustrations, and anger, we forget about how great our God is.

In our life's difficult circumstances, we miss that our God is able, that there is nothing that is impossible for Him. We often sink down to our lowest, to our deepest depression, thinking there is no way out. Certainly, this is not the TRUTH, and Satan is causing us to put our faith in ourselves (and pout over how gloomy things look), instead of keeping our eyes on Jesus, who is able to overcome all things and certainly is in control of all things.

Today, let us consider the greatness of our God—He is awesome and almighty—there is nothing that is impossible for Him. Jehovah Jireh, the Lord our provider, will go before and will take care of all our needs. Let us place our trust in Him.

Our God desires us to follow Him as He guides us to the best path for our lives.

#trustgod #letgoletgod #godisforus #godlovesus #godisfaithful #godprovides #godrestores #godisable

Monday, July 15, 2013, New York, NY

374.

> For we are God's masterpiece. He has created us anew in Christ Jesus, so we can do the good things he planned for us long ago. In those days you were living apart from Christ. You were excluded from citizenship among the people of Israel, and you did not know the covenant promises God had made to them. You lived in this world without God and without hope. But now you have been united with Christ Jesus. Once you were far away from God, but now you have been brought near to him through the blood of Christ. So now you Gentiles are no longer strangers and foreigners. You are citizens along with all of God's holy people. You are members of God's family. Together, we are his house, built on the foundation of the apostles and the prophets. And the cornerstone is Christ Jesus himself.
>
> Ephesians 2:10,12-13,19-20

Verse 10. God has a specific path for each of our lives—to do what is good. The word good may sound bland to us since there may be better words such as "great," "awesome," "excellent," or "best;" yet, throughout Scriptures we see terms like God is "good," and in Genesis, "God saw that it was good."

The word good actually signifies perfection, something excellent, best, of great(est) beauty... and those are the kinds of plans He has for each of us.

Do you accept that He created us to be His masterpiece and continues to transform us toward the "good"?

Verses 12-13. Here's the message of grace. Though we were far away, we have now been accepted because of what Jesus has done.

Verses 19-20. Here's the picture of a church. It is not you standing by yourself, but a community of believers who form the church.

It is essential for us to be involved in a believing community— wherever we may be! Otherwise, we become hypocrites when we say that we believe in God and we understand Scriptures—because certainly Satan knows the Scriptures well too and he has fooled you.

We remain in community because it is our unity of heart that demonstrates to the world that we are followers of Jesus (see John 13:35). So, love one another as the Lord has loved you. Make that your lifestyle, for this is what He calls us to, and this makes us the church.

#wearethechurch #hisgraceissufficient #loveothers #godforgives #walkwithgod #godhasaplan #trustgod

Tuesday, July 16, 2013, New York, NY

> God's purpose in all this was to use the church
> to display his wisdom in its rich variety to all the
> unseen rulers and authorities in the heavenly
> places. This was his eternal plan, which he
> carried out through Christ Jesus our Lord.
> Because of Christ and our faith in him, we can
> now come boldly and confidently into God's
> presence.

Ephesians 3:10-12

Verses 10-11. We are part of God's plan to show the world who God is. We can do that because of what Jesus has done. Jesus takes away our sins and allows us to commune with God, thereby transforming our hearts and our lives so that we may represent God through our lives.

Verse 12. We can be in a relationship with Him. Here, it talks about our Father-child relationship—where we can come boldly. It's like a kid crying in middle of service, in that quiet environment, asking for milk. Or even when you have important guests over, and your child comes and asks you for candy, cookies, or whatever they want and you will probably stop whatever you are doing to appease this child. This is the boldness that we have the privilege of. We can go any time, ask God for anything, and He hears us and puts His attention and action towards our requests.

That is what it means to be a child of God. To be able to walk in boldness knowing that we have a heavenly Father who loves us and is in control.

#sovereigngod #godlovesus #remaininhislove #walkwithgod #godforgives #trustgod #wehaveallthatweneed

Wednesday, July 17, 2013, New York, NY

376.

> Therefore I, a prisoner for serving the Lord, beg you to lead a life worthy of your calling, for you have been called by God. Always be humble and gentle. Be patient with each other, making allowance for each other's faults because of your love. Instead, let the Spirit renew your thoughts and attitudes. Put on your new nature, created to be like God—truly righteous and holy.

> Ephesians 4:1-2,23-24

The way we live our lives matter.

Some churchgoers focus on "serving the Lord"—in which, they define that they must be active in the church, handling "many" tasks / organizations / ministries. Yet, their lives outside the church are seen by others to be terrible. For example, their school grades are terrible, they are terrible employees, and they are terrible to non-believers. Yet, they act like an "angel" inside the church. No one can question them because they are doing so much in the church. Yet, like the rocky soil, burn out will occur in the long run, and their hearts may be characterized by grief and bitterness even for the work they felt they were doing for the Lord.

Such is a bad testimony of whom Jesus called us to be. We are called to be the salt and light of the world, to be filled with the Holy Spirit and to be led by Him.

Our calling is generally is accompanied by hard work, our striving (that is, being respectable in school, work, friends, family, etc), and our demonstrating Christ-likeness as we go about our daily lives, at work, at school, with friends, and even on the web. (Though we may be imperfect, people can see the changes in our lives, and how we strive to be righteous and holy).

So, let us be patient with others because our God is patient with us, as we see others grow towards becoming more Christ-like. This is the concept of unity of the Church—we all are aiming to grow to become more like Christ.

We can support each other and help others to grow. For those who have no intention of growing, we ought to pray for them and again, be patient with them. Only God is able to bring about salvation in their lives.

Let us seek transformation in our hearts. What are some things in our hearts that have hardened? Let's ask God to make us fluid like the "good soil" so that we may move as He moves.

#breakthrough #heartmatters #meaningfullife #hisgraceissufficient #letyourlifeshine #bedifferent #godprovides

Thursday, July 18, 2013, New York, NY

377.

For there is one body and one Spirit, just as you have been called to one glorious hope for the future.

Ephesians 4:4

It is a mistake to build an entrepreneurial empire for yourself if it is not in line with God's "One glorious hope for the future." We align to God's plans.

This plan of God is probably much bigger and grander than we can imagine or think. And this plan of God is good, good for you and everyone around you.

Do not go after the world's riches. Doing so without being in relationship with God thinking that you will follow His plans later in life will only lead you to be further from God's better plan for you.

Let us turn to God, and wait patiently on the Lord as we seek His guidance always.

#waitongod #turntogod #letgoletgod #heartmatters #bedifferent #notofthisworld #godhasaplan

Friday, January 10, 2020, Old Tappan, NJ USA

378.

> Imitate God, therefore, in everything you do,
> because you are his dear children. Take no part
> in the worthless deeds of evil and darkness;
> instead, expose them. And further, submit to one
> another out of reverence for Christ. This is a
> great mystery, but it is an illustration of the way
> Christ and the church are one.

Ephesians 5:1,11,21,32

Verse 1. A calling to be Christ-like.

Verse 11. Here's a struggle as we have seen in Matthew 7 to not judge others, but here, it says to expose them.

There is a misunderstanding of the concept of judging, and Christians often shy away from correction and proper rebuke. In the end, the Church would be without standards and the people would be doing as they please if the concept of judgment is not understood correctly.

As the Church, we are to judge one another! That is, believers must correct and rebuke other believers. We ought not judge non-believers, but tolerate them until they come to faith. For those who confess to believe, they need to be corrected and rebuked when out of line with the Scriptures.

Matthew 7 says that one ought to understand the standard by which one judges others, as you will also be judged by that standard. That standard is the standard of Christ. And as believers, when we get corrected or rebuked (unless it is completely out of line), we ought to accept them and thank the person for correcting us. (If the person happens to rebuke us without full understanding, we ought to "gently" help them see their flaw of understanding and restore them).

As believers, we represent Christ by upholding His perfect standard (even though we fall short—there's the grace we cling on to).

Verses 21, 32. God calls us to model unity. Christ and we, the Church, are one. The Church is one when we unite in Jesus's Lordship. A family is one when we unite in Jesus's Lordship (families are a church in itself). A church (like our ministry) is one when we unite in Jesus's Lordship. The pastoral staff is one when we unite in Jesus's Lordship. Christian fellowships, evangelism ministries, mercy ministries, your businesses, and even our own lives are one when we unite in Jesus's Lordship.

So, die to yourself and submit to one another. Model Christ. Demonstrate oneness by your humility and submission. And lead when God calls you to.

#gowhengodcalls #godforgives #godcorrects #godrestores #bedifferent #notofthisworld #hisgraceissufficient

Friday, July 19, 2013, New York, NY

379.

> For husbands, this means love your wives, just as Christ loved the church. He gave up his life for her to make her holy and clean, washed by the cleansing of God's word. He did this to present her to himself as a glorious church without a spot or wrinkle or any other blemish. Instead, she will be holy and without fault. In the same way, husbands ought to love their wives as they love their own bodies. For a man who loves his wife actually shows love for himself.
>
> Ephesians 5:25-28

Men, let us die for our wives and children.

This is the call for those who are head of families, just as Jesus, the head of the Church, does the same for us, the bride. As the groom, we are to sacrifice to enable those in our care to be holy and clean (verse 26) and to present her as a glorious church that is holy and without fault (verse 27).

We are to teach and model the right way to live. This requires us to remain close to the Word and live righteously.

Thanks be to God, for He enables us to live that way despite our failures and mistakes.

#godforgives #blessingsfromgod #walkwithgod #renewal #calling #comeholyspirit #wehaveallthatweneed

Tuesday, January 21, 2020, Saint James Parish, Jamaica

Try to please them all the time, not just when
they are watching you. As slaves of Christ, do
the will of God with all your heart. Work with
enthusiasm, as though you were working for the
Lord rather than for people. Therefore, put on
every piece of God's armor so you will be able to
resist the enemy in the time of evil. Then after
the battle you will still be standing firm. Stand
your ground, putting on the belt of truth and the
body armor of God's righteousness. For shoes,
put on the peace that comes from the Good
News so that you will be fully prepared. In
addition to all of these, hold up the shield of faith
to stop the fiery arrows of the devil. Put on
salvation as your helmet, and take the sword of
the Spirit, which is the word of God. Pray in the
Spirit at all times and on every occasion. Stay
alert and be persistent in your prayers for all
believers everywhere. And pray for me, too. Ask
God to give me the right words so I can boldly
explain God's mysterious plan that the Good
News is for Jews and Gentiles alike. I am in
chains now, still preaching this message as God's
ambassador. So pray that I will keep on speaking
boldly for him, as I should.

Ephesians 6:6-7,13-20

Verses 6-7. In all things, let us seek the will of the Lord and carry
them forward with all our hearts. Many times, we have fears of
chartering the unknown—whether unknown experiences, unknown
confrontations, and unknown circumstances. When we say "doing the
will of God," He often takes us away from our comfort zone (consider
Abraham, Moses, David, all Biblical heroes of faith—and us too!) and
puts us in places where we can only trust in Him. And in the end, this is
the test in itself, that instead of giving up, grumbling before the Lord,
and renouncing Him—we cling to Him. (BTW, He often is doing
amazing things in the background to bring about incredible results
during this time).

In these times where fear may be imminent, let us move with enthusiasm with trust that He is in control—for surely, we are working for the Lord than for the people.

Verses 13-18. Following above, this is how we cling on to God; it is by placing our trust in Jesus. As we do God's will, there will be spiritual opposition. Many will turn against us, things will go wrong, problems may arise. What should we do in this situation? run? hide? give up on God? Certainly, this scenario is similar to the temptation Jesus went through after his forty days of wilderness (see Matthew 4). Nope... you stand firm. Your trust in God does not waiver. Put on the armor of God.

Truth - check that your actions are based on His Word. If any failings, come before the Lord—for He is merciful. Then stand on His Word.

Righteousness - Be sure that your relationship with God is right, and that your dealings with and actions toward others are right. This is what it means to be righteous.

Peace - this one may be hard, especially in light of difficult circumstances—"believe" (without wavering) that God is in control. This is the Gospel—that He will walk with us, be our guide. The question that would bring us true peace in our hearts: do we really believe it? Note: this faith, this peace, is so that "you will be fully prepared" to withstand enemy's attacks.

Verse 15. Faith - trust, unrelenting, unyielding reliance on God—again to withstand enemy's attacks.

Salvation - we certainly have it, and we know the victory is ours even as we face Satan's attacks.

Sword of the Spirit - the Word, the will of God. His revealed direction for you. Go forward enthusiastically knowing that the Lord is by your side.

Verses 19-20. Speaking as someone who doesn't have it all together—I still look forward to what God has in store for me. It certainly is a journey! I know God has a plan for me in the marketplace; that is, to be influential to the people who do not know God outside the church. How that comes about, I do not know—how I will be influential? Only time will tell.

As a brother in Christ who is in need of grace and mercy, I do need your prayers, as each of you do too. As your pastor (which many of you know is a temporary role in my life's journey), I ask for your prayers that I may not cease to speak the Good News, which is the Truth (Scriptures in its entirety), and continue on in doing His will during this time of ministry. I believe this experience will enable me to proclaim God as He develops me in the marketplace.

And you too—fight the good fight. Let's enjoy the experience we have together in the now, and look forward to what God has for us. He certainly has an amazing future for you too. Let's stand amazed at what God is going to do through each of us. He is doing incredible things.

#sovereigngod #wehaveallthatweneed #befruitful #bedifferent #letyourlifeshine #noworries #makegodpriority

Saturday, July 20, 2013, New York, NY

381.

Work with enthusiasm, as though you were working for the Lord rather than for people.

Ephesians 6:7

Our lives ought to be filled with joy in all we do, because our purpose and our focus in life is to trust in His providence and walk with Him. Let us not allow our circumstances to dictate our outlooks in life. It is going to be good, because our Father is good, and He is good to us.

#godisfaithful #expectfromgod #trustgod #noworries #waitongod #restwithgod #sovereigngod #walkwithgod

Sunday, January 12, 2020, Ridgefield, NJ USA

Philippians

382.

May God our Father and the Lord Jesus Christ
give you grace and peace. And I am certain that
God, who began the good work within you, will
continue his work until it is finally finished on the
day when Christ Jesus returns. I pray that your
love will overflow more and more, and that you
will keep on growing in knowledge and
understanding. For I want you to understand
what really matters, so that you may live pure
and blameless lives until the day of Christ's
return. May you always be filled with the fruit of
your salvation - the righteous character
produced in your life by Jesus Christ - for this
will bring much glory and praise to God. For I
fully expect and hope that I will never be
ashamed, but that I will continue to be bold for
Christ, as I have been in the past. And I trust that
my life will bring honor to Christ, whether I live
or die. For to me, living means living for Christ,
and dying is even better. But if I live, I can do
more fruitful work for Christ. So I really don't
know which is better. Above all, you must live as
citizens of heaven, conducting yourselves in a
manner worthy of the Good News about Christ.
Then, whether I come and see you again or only
hear about you, I will know that you are standing
together with one spirit and one purpose,
fighting together for the faith, which is the Good
News. Don't be intimidated in any way by your
enemies. This will be a sign to them that they are
going to be destroyed, but that you are going to
be saved, even by God himself.

Verse 2. Grace and peace is used in a greeting. It shows how much each of us need it. Grace means to be forgiven even though we are undeserving.

Peace. We would think there is lack of peace only due to a recent phenomenon of technology and a fast paced world. However, people throughout the years have been in worries, fears, and lack of peace. We too can become this way.

Yet, with grace (being completely forgiven and having our past wrongs being taken away), we can be at peace (oneness, stillness, and being at rest) because of what Jesus has done.

Verse 6. God has an amazing, out-of-this-world, plans for each of our lives, and we know He will continue his discipline, train, and guide until we fulfill His plans for us.

Verses 9-11. What really matters is that our love overflows and that we keep growing (in knowledge and understanding/wisdom), that we may live pure and blameless lives. We can rely on the fruit of salvation (grace and peace), and be centered on Him (character) through our lives. This will bring much glory and praise to God.

Verse 20-22. My personal prayer: not just in the church, but in the workplace, within friends, when I go out to lunch with co-workers, may my life be a living representation of my great Lord and King. It is while I live that I can demonstrate this by the way I live, by the way I trust.

Verse 27-28. Our lives matter! Let us live in a manner that is worthy of the Good News about Christ. That is:

1. The way we live matters.

2. We must stand together with one spirit and purpose (trust in God's hierarchy, listen/obey the leaders God has set before you)

3. Fight together for faith. Be accountable and rebuke one another where needed (between believers). Help each other to remain faithful

4. Don't be afraid or fear, especially those who oppose you as you stand to do the will of God.

#trustgod #letyourlifeshine #bedifferent #loveothers #blessothers #befruitful #wearethechurch

Sunday, July 21, 2013, New York, NY

383.

> Don't be selfish; don't try to impress others. Be humble, thinking of others as better than yourselves. Don't look out only for your own interests, but take an interest in others, too. You must have the same attitude that Christ Jesus had.
>
> Philippians 2:3-5

Paradox of leadership.

A leader is someone who has a solid vision and does not waiver in it. In that sense, all Christians are to be leaders—that in the face of danger, persecution, or even temptations, we hold fast to our faith in our Lord Jesus Christ. When people doubt, we still hold.

Now, the issue is—what if people don't like what you are doing, what you want them to do, how you go about doing things—should you bend to their views? These verse says to not be selfish, but rather be humble and take an interest in others. How would you rectify that one? Does that mean that even though we feel God is telling us to go out to the streets, since others do not want to go (due to inconvenience, laziness, or just plain—"I don't think it's going to work"), we should please them and say—"ok, maybe when you are ready?"
This passage ends with, "you must have the same attitude that Christ Jesus had."

This calls us to look at Jesus' life—how He lived, and how He handled the crowd. What is amazing is that Jesus did so many things within His three years of ministry and had many crowds telling him that He should heal XYZ people, that He should be at ABC locations, and that Jesus should overtake the Roman empire and start a new kingdom.

Jesus did not comply with the crowd. Jesus focused on remaining close with the Father and those close to him. Even in the midst of busyness (crowds gathering constantly), he left for the secret place. He understood that His secret relationship with God mattered, and that was His source of strength.

Then, as the Lord guided Him, He followed and did only as He saw the Father doing things (John 5:19). And we too should do that—as leaders, as Christians. Stay close to our Father, and do as He guides you.

This in fact answers the questions I began with (read v. 3 and 4 again). We are not being selfish by trusting the Father (we don't need to worry about impressing others, because we are just doing as we are told), and certainly, we are not looking to our own interests, but rather being obedient to the Father so that others may see the good results for them (for example, Jesus healed others because that was what the Father was doing—that is how Jesus took interest in others, by being obedient to God's guidance).

#walkwithgod #listentogod #obeygod #blessothers #loveothers #godhasaplan

Monday, July 22, 2013, New York, NY

384.

> Though he was God, he did not think of equality
> with God as something to cling to. Instead, he
> gave up his divine privileges; he took the humble
> position of a slave and was born as a human
> being. When he appeared in human form, he
> humbled himself in obedience to God and died a
> criminal's death on a cross. Therefore, God
> elevated him to the place of highest honor and
> gave him the name above all other names,

> Philippians 2:6-9

Giving up our privileges (our skills, talents, resources) for others.

As imitators of Jesus, we can read verses 6-7 as,
Though I am blessed with _____ (substitute the blank with
what God has gifted you), I do not think of it as something to cling to. I
give up my privileges and will take the position of a slave.

With that mindset, God elevates us and enables us to live the life
of influence, which reflects how Jesus lived.

#blessingsfromgod #abandonall #blessothers #givetoothers #loveothers #bethankful

Tuesday, January 14, 2020, Fort Lee, NJ USA

385.

> Whatever happens, my dear brothers and sisters , rejoice in the Lord. I never get tired of telling you these things, and I do it to safeguard your faith. For we who worship by the Spirit of God are the ones who are truly circumcised. We rely on what Christ Jesus has done for us. We put no confidence in human effort, Yes, everything else is worthless when compared with the infinite value of knowing Christ Jesus my Lord. For his sake I have discarded everything else, counting it all as garbage, so that I could gain Christ and become one with him. I no longer count on my own righteousness through obeying the law; rather, I become righteous through faith in Christ. For God's way of making us right with himself depends on faith. I don't mean to say that I have already achieved these things or that I have already reached perfection. But I press on to possess that perfection for which Christ Jesus first possessed me. For I have told you often before, and I say it again with tears in my eyes, that there are many whose conduct shows they are really enemies of the cross of Christ. They are headed for destruction. Their god is their appetite, they brag about shameful things, and they think only about this life here on earth.

> Philippians 3:1,3,8-9,12,18-19

Verse 1. Whether we go through hardships, difficulties—even as we follow the will of the Lord—rejoice. This is hard, especially when we feel overwhelmed with life. Let us learn to let go and trust God—He is in control. When we do, we can rejoice even when things are not getting done to our "perfect" standards.

Verse 3. When God asks as we enter heaven's gates, He would ask us, what have you done in your life that you should be allowed into heaven. Many of us may scramble and say, I did many good works, I was the worship leader, I was the pastor, I shared the gospel and many people came to faith, I did well in school/work that I represented you correctly, I served the poor and gave them food to eat. Then we would realize that our works do not measure up.

The right answer is, I placed all my faith in Jesus and on what He has done. (period).

And out of that overjoy (that rejoicing from verse 1), I acted to worship, to preach, to share the gospel, to help the poor, etc. But I have only done as You have guided my heart, I have certainly *done* nothing to get me into heaven. It was Jesus that made the way. =)

Verse 8-9, 12. Even the Apostle Paul wasn't perfect in faith. He is saying he continued to grow in that joy (despite persecutions, things not working out the way he planned, etc) but there were also times when he failed. Yet, he was growing—toward that "perfection." We are growing too! So, let us not be critical of each other, but allow one another to fail because that is the only way to our growth.

If we hold a perfectionist mindset and feel that we must do everything right, we will not move in freedom, but rather be tied up with the burdens of self-improvement, and inaction until we get it just right, which will never happen. This is the opposite of obedience as the Lord guides you. So, let it go . . . and trust. This is the path to our growth toward perfection.

Verse 18-19. During our life on earth, what do we need to accomplish before we die? We often are in a rush to get this, and that, and accomplish something. As we continue to live out that lifestyle, we burn out, grow weary, and eventually, may not want to do it any more. It may come even to points of avoiding others because they are getting in the way of our accomplishing tasks. We may become bitter at the world because our lives are so hectic.

When this happens to us, let us instead picture eternity. To get something done in consideration of eternity, how much time do we have? What are some values that you wish to take with you after our finite lives on earth? Do you want to take with you that bitterness or the rushed heart? or rather, would you like to take the peace and joy of knowing God, which therefore connects you with others in community?

Working in a rush lowers the value of relationships, which is why Jesus came to die for us. Do you only think about your life here on earth? or do you have eternity in mind?

#walkinfaith #wehaveallthatweneed #wearethechurch #letyourlifeshine #noworries #bedifferent #meaningfullife

Tuesday, July 23, 2013, New York, NY

386.

> Therefore, my dear brothers and sisters, stay
> true to the Lord. I love you and long to see you,
> dear friends, for you are my joy and the crown I
> receive for my work.

Philippians 4:1

Paul calls us to remain true—to not be fake and not seeking to be acceptable by others, that is, to be a people-pleaser, one who is not truly him/herself.

The rest of the passage is about Paul's expression of joy. It is because of others, and may it be the same for you who are reading this.

#loveothers #blessothers #bemerciful #calling #walkinfaith #heartmatters #bethankful #comeasyouare

Wednesday, July 24, 2013, New York, NY

Colossians

387.

> For through him God created everything in the
> heavenly realms and on earth. He made the
> things we can see and the things we cannot
> see—such as thrones, kingdoms, rulers, and
> authorities in the unseen world. Everything was
> created through him and for him. He existed
> before anything else, and he holds all creation
> together. Christ is also the head of the church,
> which is his body. He is the beginning, supreme
> over all who rise from the dead. So he is first in
> everything. For God in all his fullness was
> pleased to live in Christ,

Colossians 1:16-19

Our businesses, our families, all that we may treasure or hold personal, they are built through Him and is for Him (verse 16). He holds all things together for his purposes. They are less about our doing or the results we have produced, but it is more about His purposes and plans and what He does through us.

He is our Head (we are the body, the Church) and He is pleased to dwell amongst us. So:

1. Let us not worry about the results of our current pursuits. Let Him handle it. It's His, and we are simply partakers of the infinite treasures that God our Father has for us, both for eternity and even today.

2. Let us thank God and give Him glory for all the results (accomplishments, our wives/children, etc) He has given us thus far.

#bethankful #mygodissobig #godprovides #godisourstrength #godisforus #submittogod #noworries

Friday, January 17, 2020, George Washington Bridge, NY

388.

> And now, just as you accepted Christ Jesus as your Lord, you must continue to follow him. Let your roots grow down into him, and let your lives be built on him. Then your faith will grow strong in the truth you were taught, and you will overflow with thankfulness.
>
> Colossians 2:6-7

Today's passage is a lead in to how we can be less legalistic, since being so does not help with conquering a person's evil desires (verse 23). We can wait expectantly for tomorrow's verses! For today: Growth.

How does growth work for us? It's by our dependence on Him, it is by our faith. Today, I encourage you to slow down, and even stop. Do not read today's reflection so quickly—but stop, and ask—based on where I am today in my life, my current thinking, my week, how can I depend on Him? Are you centered on Him? Is your life being built around Him? Is your life about Him (or are you tied up around your worries)?

Let your roots grow down into Him, and let your lives be built on him. Come find rest in Him, and you will grow in faith, find joy, and overflow in thankfulness.

#bethankful #letyourlifeshine #keepgoing #wehaveallthatweneed #pathsstraight #walkinfaith #walkwithgod

Friday, July 26, 2013, New York, NY

389.

> Since you have been raised to new life with
> Christ, set your sights on the realities of heaven,
> where Christ sits in the place of honor at God's
> right hand. Think about the things of heaven, not
> the things of earth.

Colossians 3:1-2

Life's paradox

How to not be legalistic? Look above.

How to stop being selfish and die to self? Stop trying, and look above.

How to be humble? Stop thinking about it, and look above.

Let your focuses in life be on what God desires. Isn't that a bit hard to accept? Many people may think that being non-legalistic is to just let things be and do whatever "feels" good. Certainly, this is allowed as a Christian (see 1Corinthians 10:23), but it is not the way we ought to live as lovers of Christ.

Our foremost goal should be to be in good relationship with God; that is, to commune with Him, and know what He desires of us. Then follow.

By continuing to look above, we are no longer legalistic, but walking in His ways, which leads us to softened heart and love toward others (the rest of this chapter).

Today, let us look to Him and consider the good things He is doing.

#lookup #honorgod #notofthisworld #breakthrough #hisgraceissufficient #wearethechurch #noreligion

Saturday, July 27, 2019, New York, NY

Put on your new nature, and be renewed as you learn to know your Creator and become like him. In this new life, it doesn't matter if you are a Jew or a Gentile, circumcised or uncircumcised, barbaric, uncivilized, slave, or free. Christ is all that matters, and he lives in all of us. Since God chose you to be the holy people he loves, you must clothe yourselves with tenderhearted mercy, kindness, humility, gentleness, and patience. Make allowance for each other's faults, and forgive anyone who offends you. Remember, the Lord forgave you, so you must forgive others. Above all, clothe yourselves with love, which binds us all together in perfect harmony.

Colossians 3:10-14

Life transformation after meeting Christ leads us to become like Jesus.

It is available for anyone (whether Jew or Gentile, Korean, Chinese, Caucasian, or dark), and all that matters is Christ.

Our highest calling is love, through discipleship, which occurs through deep relationships over time in small groups.

As we are changed into Christ's image, let us encourage one another to meet often and share lives together.

#meaningfullife #wearethechurch #blessothers #loveothers #lifetransformation #letyourlifeshine #notofthisworld

Wednesday, January 22, 2020, Jamaica, Jamaica

391.

> Masters, be just and fair to your slaves.
> Remember that you also have a Master—in
> heaven.
>
> Colossians 4:1

Our employees are brothers and sisters whom God loves.

In a culture where more work is expected in understaffed environments, let us not follow the trends of overburdening the people who work for us. As much as family and other personal pursuits are important to us, let us rather be enablers of their success. Remember, our reward is from God above.

#godprovides #godisenough #godlovesus #loveothers #bemerciful #blessothers #honorgod
Thursday, January 23, 2020, New York, NY USA

392.

> Live wisely among those who are not believers,
> and make the most of every opportunity.
>
> Colossians 4:5

Keyword here is "among."

Many of us feel we ought to look "holy" in the church and in front of other church members. This will ensure that others will consider you as a good Christian, at least in the Christian circles. This is foolish! Often these same people live unrighteous (not right toward God and others) lives outside the church thinking they have done their duty for the week by attending church on the Lord's Day.

"Among" tells us our lives ought to be attractive outside the church. In our workplaces, in our schools, amongst our friends, even online—we live in the world amongst others, but are not of it.

May our lives be so attractive that people wonder what is "wrong" with us. May we live out lives demonstrating love when the world lacks it. Let us be smiling while others in the world may be full of struggles. Let them question our joyful lives so that we may answer them and walk with them on how they may come to know, and accept Jesus.

#notofthisworld #letyourlifeshine #wearethechurch #noreligion #loveconquersall #relationshipsmatter

Sunday, July 28, 2013, New York, NY

1Thessalonians

393.

We always thank God for all of you and pray for
you constantly.

1Thessalonians 1:2

Prayer for one another occurs because of already-built deep relationships.

The only reason people are able to pray for one another is because they know what the other person is up to, where s/he is heading, and needs. Such lives are only shared through a relationship that has been built over time.

There may be some exceptions, but

1. People will not pray for you outside of built relationships over time (nor will you pray for them sincerely over brief encounters). And just like the lame person who could not get to the water for healing, we need each other to cover for our weaknesses. When we feel we don't need others, it may be pride pulling you from the Body.

2. Prayer within relationships are effective (consider James 5:14-16). This calls for deeper relationships over time where

A) You are able to go to one another when you need prayer and support and

B) Be there for others when you are well. (Recurring, frequent small groups).

#bethereforoneanother #loveothers #blessothers #trustgod #expectfromgod #walkinfaith #wehaveallthatweneed

Friday, January 24, 2020, Fort Lee, NJ USA

394.

> For when we brought you the Good News, it was
> not only with words but also with power, for the
> Holy Spirit gave you full assurance that what we
> said was true. And you know of our concern for
> you from the way we lived when we were with
> you.

1Thessalonians 1:5

It is interesting how passages relate to our conversations during our weekend gatherings. Regarding evangelism:

1. "the Holy Spirit gave you full assurance" (listeners agree the message is true as the Holy Spirit leads them). God is in control on who is receptive to the Word and will handle the when and the where. Our goal of evangelism is to simply share the news when timing is appropriate. Prior to doing so, we ought to focus on building the relationships.

2. Note Paul's words: "the way we lived when we were with you." He is saying that it is about how we live our lives, whether in our workplaces, schools, amongst our friends, online, etc. How we live is what attracts others to wonder and ask about why we live the way we do. That is the opens door to our sharing the Gospel.

3. "The Good News... also with power." The Gospel has the power to transform lives and circumstances. Many people may feel that there is no power in the Word, no power in our trust in God, and our worship becomes empty and religious. However, those who know that power recognize that the Word of God can transform us and its listeners in amazing ways.

"Evangelism" happens to be a taboo in today's church environment, because many people think it is a hard thing. We may picture it as handing out fliers at a supermarket for an hour of fruitless labor. We may also cringe at the thought of speaking to a person one-on-one, where we don't know what to say, and regardless, the person does not respond favorably—and the whole interaction makes us feel like a failure.

Evangelism is simply sharing the Good News, and Christians should practice how to share the basic Gospel (see https://www.prayertents.com/gospel101).

Prior to going out and taking on any activities, build a relationships with others, those outside the church. God has placed you where you are today so you can build relationships with those around you. And that is His calling for you—may you be fruitful in your relationships and how you live your life.

#calling #befruitful #letyourlifeshine #relationshipsmatter #bedifferent #notofthisworld #noreligion

Monday, July 29, 2013, New York, NY

395.

> For we speak as messengers approved by God to be entrusted with the Good News. Our purpose is to please God, not people. He alone examines the motives of our hearts.
>
> 1Thessalonians 2:4

Today, as I am reading, I was thinking about some teaching points I can share here. The Spirit reminds me that I need the Word too, so I am just soaking it in.

You too—as you read, ask the Lord to use the Word to guide your life, grant you peace, and be the center of our hearts.

As I read the passage, I am grateful to God that He has never failed to keep me pushing forward despite the busyness and perhaps even craziness of all facets of my life (work, family, church, etc).

If I picture myself maybe 10 years ago, maybe even 5 years ago, I wonder if I would have had the faith to keep pushing forward. By this, I know I have been growing in faith, and I can walk through storms and difficulties because He has proven Himself faithful over time, especially through my walks with Him.

I pray that I'll continue to speak the truth, not out of flattery, or for my self-recognition—but for the glory of God, the glory of the only One who is worthy of our praise. Soli Deo Gloria.

#honorgod #comeasyouare #turntogod #walkwithgod #walkinfaith #pathsstraight #makegodpriority

Tuesday, July 30, 2013, New York, NY

396.

> Never once did we try to win you with flattery, as you well know. And God is our witness that we were not pretending to be your friends just to get your money! As for human praise, we have never sought it from you or anyone else.
>
> 1Thessalonians 2:5-6

Offering and Money.

These verses tell us how we should view offerings and money. As pastors, elders and people in other leadership roles in the church, we must remember that our purpose is not to flatter or to make ourselves look better because of what we speak, how we deliver the message, or how we operate.

Our purpose is not human praise, but approval from God in what He has called us to do. As members of the Body, let us be grateful that we have an opportunity to offer things that are of importance to us. Let us be grateful that we have offering baskets in the church so that we may offer something that is valuable and necessary in our lives. If there were no offering baskets, that would mean that we would have no opportunity to give back what God has given us.

Another way to view this would be the reason why we have worked for throughout the week. For whom were we earning and doing the work? Was your work for the money or for God? Our lives are not for human praise. The ability to be able to offer is also to operate as the feet, hand, legs, or whatever we may have been called... for the entire Body. Let us be thankful that our part is functioning and that we are able to also care for other parts of the Body that may not be as functional.

Offerings remind us that we are part of the greater body.

In particular, as Tentmakers, Businesspersons for Christ, let us be responsible and lovers of others around us.

Since God has given us the ability to cover for the costs of *entire* works of God, such as church projects or mission work, we may sometimes feel that we should up the resources/money/etc. However, we also must recognize that by doing so, we prevent others from offering. For example, let's suppose a mission activity requires $600, and that is very easy for us to cover. Yet, to others, $20 is the most they can offer based on their situations. Your paying the entire $600 prevents others from serving and you would not be operating out of community of Christ. You may in fact be operating out of pride (see Luke 18:9-14).

Even though we may have, let us discern and even let go of our pride to encourage others to contribute. This is especially important in missions. The people to whom we are preaching Christ may place their trust on you (or your church collectively) instead of God as you just throw money at them. They will not grow in discipleship and put their trust in God, but rather look to the "wealthy" to keep covering their costs and needs. Instead, help them to offer what they have. We can do this by discerning, living amongst them over extended time, and not treating them as a business project where throwing money may help. This is how we place love before money, or God before the world.

Let us be thankful. Let us continue to enable others to contribute and take part in the body of Christ as we too have been called. It is not for human praise, but as God directs us.

#wearethechurch #makegodpriority #honorgod #letyourlifeshine #notofthisworld #loveothers #blessothers

Saturday, January 25, 2020, Old Tappan, NJ USA

397.

> And we sent Timothy to visit you. He is our brother and God's co-worker in proclaiming the Good News of Christ. We sent him to strengthen you, to encourage you in your faith, and to keep you from being shaken by the troubles you were going through. But you know that we are destined for such troubles.
>
> 1Thessalonians 3:2-3

Be ready to be sent.

These verses challenge me quite a bit. If people needed strengthening,

1) Would others select me for it? Am I generally an encourager that strengthens others?

2) Would I be ready to strengthen others? Am I prepared and good to go?

Let us practice continually strengthening and encouraging one another so that when time comes, we are able to do the same for those who are in need of that support.

#loveothers #blessothers #bethereforoneanother #relationshipsmatter #godisourstrength #beavailable

Sunday, January 26, 2020, Ridgefield, NJ USA

398.

> Even while we were with you, we warned you
> that troubles would soon come - and they did, as
> you well know. That is why, when I could bear it
> no longer, I sent Timothy to find out whether
> your faith was still strong. I was afraid that the
> tempter had gotten the best of you and that our
> work had been useless.

1Thessalonians 3:4-5

Remaining strong, in midst of struggles, busyness, or even complacency.

Any of the above can cause us to fall into temptation. In midst of such things, let us remain in the Lord in trust, in dependence, in submission, and in obedience.

He is in control, and He is for our good, for He certainly loves us and desires the best for us. Let us remain in Him and follow.

#weareforgivenandfree #comeasyouare #trustgod #letgoletgod #sovereigngod #submittogod #trustgod #feargod

Wednesday, July 31, 2013, New York, NY

Finally, dear brothers and sisters, we urge you in the name of the Lord Jesus to live in a way that pleases God, as we have taught you. You live this way already, and we encourage you to do so even more. Then each of you will control his own body and live in holiness and honor - But we don't need to write to you about the importance of loving each other, for God himself has taught you to love one another. Make it your goal to live a quiet life, minding your own business and working with your hands, just as we instructed you before. Then people who are not Christians will respect the way you live, and you will not need to depend on others. And now, dear brothers and sisters, we want you to know what will happen to the believers who have died so you will not grieve like people who have no hope. For since we believe that Jesus died and was raised to life again, we also believe that when Jesus returns, God will bring back with him the believers who have died. We tell you this directly from the Lord: We who are still living when the Lord returns will not meet him ahead of those who have died. For the Lord himself will come down from heaven with a commanding shout, with the voice of the archangel, and with the trumpet call of God. First, the Christians who have died will rise from their graves. Then, together with them, we who are still alive and remain on the earth will be caught up in the clouds to meet the Lord in the air. Then we will be with the Lord forever. So encourage each other with these words.

1Thessalonians 4:1,4,9,11-18

Let us:

-   Be pleasing to God (v. 1)

- Live in holiness and honor (v. 4)

- Love one another (v. 9)

- Live a quiet life (and not be a cumberance to others) (v. 11)

- Work with your hands (be diligent) (v. 11)

- be respected by the way that we live, especially for those who do not believe in Jesus yet (v. 12)

- Live this way as we look forward to the perfect future. (v. 13-18)

These are the crux of the *To One Another Ministries* that we live to please God by seeking holiness, and out of the love that we receive from Him to be unto others. And thus, may our lives be attractive to all people.

Certainly some of us are attractive in our services, but truly, God is checking our hearts, which lead to how we live our lives outside the church. Let us ask the Lord to cleanse our hearts so that we may be pure in His sight, and may our hearts be unto others.

#letyourlifeshine #bedifferent #notofthisworld #lookup #narrowpath #honorgod #abandonall #calling #renewal

Thursday, August 1, 2013, New York, NY

400.

> God's will is for you to be holy, so stay away from all sexual sin. Then each of you will control his own body and live in holiness and honor - Never harm or cheat a Christian brother in this matter by violating his wife, for the Lord avenges all such sins, as we have solemnly warned you before. God has called us to live holy lives, not impure lives.

> 1Thessalonians 4:3-4,6-7

Holy Living for Men of God.

Verse 7 points to our calling to live holy lives, where holy means to be set apart or different from the rest of the world. Without holiness, we become the people of the world and certainly look that way in sight of others.

For men, we have special instructions in being holy. This holiness centers around loving others. It points to how men may 1) love other women, 2) love his wife, and 3) love other men.

1. Men may love all sisters in Christ by considering them to belong to their husbands, or future husbands. With that mindset, married men ought to turn away from desires toward any women as God has given them the person to love in your life.

    Unmarried men ought to consider a sister for marriage, and if not, should protect them as someone else's wife (or someone else's future wife).

2. Verse 4 refers to wife as "own body" by being faithful (in body AND in thought/heart). He upholds their holiness and honor for both him and his wife (or as they are *one* through marriage).

3. Verse 6. We love our brothers by not having lustful desires for their wives (or future wives)

A short way to remember all the permutations above, is to simply love your one wife. For unmarried men, love your one future wife, and build up your heart to love that one person.

Let our hearts not go toward any other, but the one person with whom God has given us to be united and become one. This union refers us to our sole love for God, despite many "options" that the world seems to offer us. That is Satan showing offering you the world for your soul and allegiance.

Let us be holy (be single-minded), as our God is holy.

#remaininhislove #comeholyspirit #lookup #bedifferent #notofthisworld #letyourlifeshine #noreligion

Monday, January 27, 2020, New York, NY USA

> So be on your guard, not asleep like the others.
> Stay alert and be clearheaded. Always be joyful.
> Never stop praying. Be thankful in all
> circumstances, for this is God's will for you who
> belong to Christ Jesus. Do not scoff at
> prophecies, but test everything that is said. Hold
> on to what is good.
>
> 1Thessalonians 5:6,16-18,20-21

Verse 6 says to be clearheaded. How? This is certainly not by being overworked and only by being solely focused on the details of the work at hand.

This relates to the story where Martha is cleaning and preparing for guests while Mary is just hanging out with Jesus. Martha gets angry and demands that Mary help her, while Jesus commends Mary for doing the better thing (see Luke 10:40-42).

What that means for us is: let us learn to rest, be with Jesus, and think bigger.

Big picture thinking, instead of just doing the work. Ask yourself why you are doing the work. Assess continuously if the right work is being done or if you are just being a busybody (see 2Thessalonians 3:11).

Many of us, even in our times when we do not have much that needs to be accomplished, try to remain busy in our minds. Let it go and accept it as an invitation to spend time with the Lord.

If your life is hectic and crazy busy, Jesus offers an invitation to stop, and spend time with God. Remember, Jesus had to do this on a daily basis despite the many crowds that kept following him.

Verses 16-18.

- Be joyful = let go of your worries.

- Never stop praying = stay in a deep relationship with God. Intentionally spend time with God.

- Be thankful always = know that God is in control and trust that all He does is for our good

Verses 20-21. Hold on to the dreams God has given you and continue to grow in them. Inquire God along the way regarding which way we ought to go. Stay strong everyone!

#letgoletgod #restwithgod #walkwithgod #turntogod #submittogod #trustgod #godprovides #comeholyspirit

Friday, August 2, 2013, New York, NY

2Thessalonians

402.

And God will use this persecution to show his
justice and to make you worthy of his Kingdom,
for which you are suffering.

2Thessalonians 1:5

Our sufferings are for our good.

We have a good Father who is control of everything, and He
loves us! Persevere brothers and sisters, as our current struggles are only
for our good.

#keepgoing #remaininhislove #hisgraceissufficient #wehaveallthatweneed #bethereforoneanother #trustgod

Thursday, January 30, 2020, Leonia, NJ USA

403.

And God will provide rest for you who are being
persecuted and also for us when the Lord Jesus
appears from heaven. He will come with his
mighty angels, in flaming fire, bringing judgment
on those who don't know God and on those who
refuse to obey the Good News of our Lord
Jesus. They will be punished with eternal
destruction, forever separated from the Lord
and from his glorious power. When he comes on
that day, he will receive glory from his holy
people - praise from all who believe. And this
includes you, for you believed what we told you
about him. So we keep on praying for you,
asking our God to enable you to live a life
worthy of his call. May he give you the power to
accomplish all the good things your faith
prompts you to do. Then the name of our Lord
Jesus will be honored because of the way you
live, and you will be honored along with him. This
is all made possible because of the grace of our
God and Lord, Jesus Christ.

2Thessalonians 1:7-12

When going through difficult stages of our lives, just as the
Thessalonians were going through, know that He will provide for you
just as He did for them. Paul encouraged them to remain in God in
unwavering trust, and the call is the same for us today.

Our actions would be simple prayers of dependence on His
sovereignty. Consider the difficulties we experience—it is a way for us to
grow in faith—because ultimately, God desires to do something amazing
through our lives, much more amazing than we can picture. To get
there, we must trust and obey through the difficulties instead of running
from them.

So let us trust and depend on Him, and rather be thankful.

May He give us the power to accomplish all the good things our faith prompts us to do (v. 11).

#trustgod #godprovides #godisourstrength #letgoletgod #hisgraceissufficient #noworries #narrowpath

Saturday, August 3, 2013, New York, NY

404.

> Don't be so easily shaken or alarmed by those
> who say that the day of the Lord has already
> begun. Don't believe them, even if they claim to
> have had a spiritual vision, a revelation, or a
> letter supposedly from us. With all these things
> in mind, dear brothers and sisters, stand firm and
> keep a strong grip on the teaching we passed on
> to you both in person and by letter.
>
> 2Thessalonians 2:2,15

If you have been following the message of the letters to Thessalonica, it is about suffering for the Lord, and Paul has been encouraging them to stand strong. Us too—let us remain strong in our faith in Jesus Christ our Lord.

One of the ways the people tempted Christians in Thessalonica is by saying, did not Jesus come already? Why do you suffer if He already did? Jesus really is not the Son of God, and since you are suffering, God really doesn't love you or care about you, so why bother with your beliefs? I know at times, we too may feel that way, but Apostle Paul encourages us to hold firmly to the faith we have because these accusations are simply not true.

In God's time, we will enter into a perfect place of joy, where there is no sorrow and no more pain. Until then, we will face difficulties, struggles, and afflictions in our lives. So, take heart!

Even in the midst of our struggles, our Lord is with us in His perfect sovereignty. We can rest because He is in control.

With all these things in mind, dear brothers and sisters, stand firm and keep a strong grip on the teaching we passed on to you both in person and by letter. (v. 15)

#relationshipsmatter #bethereforoneanother #sovereigngod #trustgod #walkwithgod #waitongod #godisforus

Sunday, August 4, 2013, New York, NY

405.

> May the Lord lead your hearts into a full understanding and expression of the love of God and the patient endurance that comes from Christ. We certainly had the right to ask you to feed us, but we wanted to give you an example to follow. Yet we hear that some of you are living idle lives, refusing to work and meddling in other people's business. We command such people and urge them in the name of the Lord Jesus Christ to settle down and work to earn their own living.
>
> 2Thessalonians 3:5,9,11-12

Verse 5. Following the story, Thessalonians have been going through much suffering and persecution. End result of all sufferings, difficulties, and struggles for the faithful is the full understanding and expression of the love of God.

Not that God wants us to suffer, but He desires our hearts to know His full and amazing love for us. So, as we go through the difficulties in our lives, know that He is working both outside of us as well as the inside of us.

In the end, we will be satisfied because of what He has been doing. Stay strong!

Verses 9, 11-12. Paul ends this letter telling us to live exemplary lives. In particular, he says to be respectful to those around us because of our faith.

Here, we see people who are unwilling to pull their load and rather complain much. What causes people to complain? It's because they are bored, it is because they are not actively committed, and it is because they do not wish to be responsible but rather blame.

Certainly, people who often complain the most are those that are not involved. They may say, "If s/he did this, if s/he did that, everything would be better!" Yet, Paul calls us to get involved and actively work! Only such people should be bringing forth ways to improve the situation, and actively work toward that goal. The people who complain are simply talkers that take no action and are people who are unwilling to take the stand and be responsible for the things they complain about.

As Christians, we need to ask, are we willing to expend time/effort to help out? If not, we should remain quiet.

In the end, live a life of respect as Christians. This means to keep up with our grades, do right unto others, do what you are to do in your workplace, care for your employees/subordinates as owners/managers because of our love for Christ.

We are called to be the salt and light of this world. To do so, may our lives be examples for others to follow.

#letyourlifeshine #befruitful #wearethechurch #loveconquersall #honorgod #letmywordsbefew #loveothers

Monday, August 5, 2013, New York, NY

1Timothy

406.

This letter is from Paul, an apostle of Christ Jesus, appointed by the command of God our Savior and Christ Jesus, who gives us hope. Don't let them waste their time in endless discussion of myths and spiritual pedigrees. These things only lead to meaningless speculations, which don't help people live a life of faith in God. The purpose of my instruction is that all believers would be filled with love that comes from a pure heart, a clear conscience, and genuine faith. But some people have missed this whole point. They have turned away from these things and spend their time in meaningless discussions. I thank Christ Jesus our Lord, who has given me strength to do his work. He considered me trustworthy and appointed me to serve him, even though I used to blaspheme the name of Christ. In my insolence, I persecuted his people. But God had mercy on me because I did it in ignorance and unbelief. Oh, how generous and gracious our Lord was! He filled me with the faith and love that come from Christ Jesus. Cling to your faith in Christ, and keep your conscience clear. For some people have deliberately violated their consciences; as a result, their faith has been shipwrecked.

1Timothy 1:1,4-6,12-14,19

Here starts the letter of Paul to a young Christian leader named Timothy. You will see that just like any of us who want to live for the Lord, Timothy felt much pressure from his culture, his peers, and his environment. In that place, Paul encourages Timothy to live right, and may we also aim to do the same.

As you read, also consider the concept of Church. How should we be as a whole?

Verses 4-6, 19. In your conversations, let there be testimonies of how God is doing amazing things in your life and your circumstances. For this to happen, you must also be growing in your relationship with God, and in your knowledge of the Word. Without them, you would have no testimonies to share because you would be attributing all your activities and results to yourself without acknowledging God.

Verses 12-14. As we grow, let us never forget the grace that we have received. Know that Paul can boast about his scholarships and his all his past training and experience, but he does not, and rather points to Jesus, His grace, and what He has done.

We too are well equipped simply because of who He is and His acceptance of us into His family. When confused about life or feeling weak and powerless, know that He has given us the strength to do His work. It is not about us, but His strength that is in us. Trust and follow.

#mygodissobig #godprovides #wehaveallthatweneed #letgoletgod #godisforus #godisourstrength #godisenough

Tuesday, August 6, 2013, New York, NY

407.

> He gave his life to purchase freedom for everyone. This is the message God gave to the world at just the right time. In every place of worship, I want men to pray with holy hands lifted up to God, free from anger and controversy. For women who claim to be devoted to God should make themselves attractive by the good things they do.
>
> 1Timothy 2:6,8,10

Pray for all.

Ask God to help them, intercede on their behalf, and give thanks for them, pray also for kings and those in authority Rest of the chapter is regarding worship:

1. It is about God, not about us (verse 6)

2. Therefore, lift hands up to God with a clear heart (not angry or with conflicts) (verse 8)

3. Don't dress in such a flashy way to make others adore you; rather, make God be the center (verse 10)

#letyourlifeshine #sovereigngod #rightwithgod #blessothers #loveothers #bemerciful #relationshipsmatter

Wednesday, August 7, 2013, New York, NY

408.

> This is a trustworthy saying: "If someone aspires
> to be an elder, he desires an honorable position."

1Timothy 3:1

Today's passage is regarding church leadership. Many people seek titles and positions, but true servants are those that are able to function without them. Such people would put in the time and efforts because they believe and operates as the Lord directs them. They do not do the work because their title or positions dictate it.

Questions for today—are you worthy of being a deacon or an elder? Would you faithfully serve the Lord, listen, obey, and love? Or would you seek your comforts, your selfish pursuits, and demand that the church be run the way you are used to? Would you submit to the Holy Spirit?

Put into practice now the way you believe a deacon or an elder should act. Those who unable to do that now, when given such positions, will do exactly what they are used to doing—which is to demand things out of their own personal pursuits. They are blind to see what God desires and will seek their own selfish gain. (Isn't that what we see in our churches today from elders and deacons who may be causing dissension in the Church?)

Many churches fail because of such leadership. You are a leader because of whom God has called you to be. Will you lead following the heart of the Lord?

#letyourlifeshine #remaininhislove #wearethechurch #calling #heartmatters #bedifferent #makegodpriority

Thursday, August 8, 2013, New York, NY

409.

> So an elder must be a man whose life is above reproach. He must be faithful to his wife. He must exercise self-control, live wisely, and have a good reputation. He must enjoy having guests in his home, and he must be able to teach.

1Timothy 3:2

Elder (a pastor, any person called by God, you!) must:

1. Be faithful to his family

2. Have self-control

3. Live wisely

4. Have a good reputation

5. Enjoy having guests in our home

6. Be able to teach

    Let us be like that.

#loveothers #blessothers #givetoothers #letyourlifeshine #wearethechurch #bedifferent #makegodpriority

Tuesday, February 4, 2020, Old Tappan, NJ USA

410.

> These people are hypocrites and liars, and their consciences are dead. Until I get there, focus on reading the Scriptures to the church, encouraging the believers, and teaching them. Do not neglect the spiritual gift you received through the prophecy spoken over you when the elders of the church laid their hands on you. Keep a close watch on how you live and on your teaching. Stay true to what is right for the sake of your own salvation and the salvation of those who hear you.
>
> 1Timothy 4:2,13-14,16

So-called Christians who are not accepted by God as His followers are

1. Hypocrites. People who do not do what they say or people do not do what they know is the right thing to do

2. Liars. People who distort the truth for self gain.

Rather, rightful Christians are:

1. People who do not get swayed by false information because of their continual study of Scriptures.

2. People who know the truth in their heart to encourage and teach others

3. People who are humble in mind and recognize that even when one is weak, the blessings and providences of God carry them, such as in laying of hands.

#pathsstraight #wehaveallthatweneed #turntogod #walkwithgod #listentogod #bedifferent #letyourlifeshine

Wednesday, February 5, 2020, New York, NY USA

411.

> Don't let anyone think less of you because you are young. Be an example to all believers in what you say, in the way you live, in your love, your faith, and your purity. Keep a close watch on how you live and on your teaching. Stay true to what is right for the sake of your own salvation and the salvation of those who hear you.
>
> 1Timothy 4:12,16

Deceptive spirits and teachings that come from demons.

If you look at the society today, note that it is pulling us toward many different directions. It says we need to be fit and beautiful, eat healthy, have a good job, make lots of money, need a nice car, nice house, etc. etc.

But in the end, we only need one thing—Jesus.

Idolatry is anything that turns us away from God, and such a deception is what the world presents to us. Do not be fooled to believe that being more fast-paced is the way to success. Instead, slow down, and stop if necessary and give God glory.

Verse 12. This is a verse I enjoyed ever since I was young. It is not through our strength amazing things happen. No, it is by God's mighty hands that *He* does amazing things.

In that respect, He can certainly use us no matter how young we may be, and despite our inexperience, still do mighty and awesome things.

Trust in Him and don't shrink back regardless of your age. During your youth, "be an example to all believers in what you say, in the way you live, in your love, your faith, and your purity."

Verse 16. Be sure to speak the truth and stay close to the Word of God. Also, be careful how you live. The way you live your life matters. It is by your life that others will come to know God.

#letyourlifeshine #bedifferent #notofthisworld #remaininhislove #lookup #trustgod #gowhengodcalls

Saturday, August 10, 2013, New York, NY

412.

In the same way, the good deeds of some people are obvious. And the good deeds done in secret will someday come to light.

1Timothy 5:25

Doing good in secret.

Would you do it if no one notices the benefits you give to others? No one will notice. No one will care. Perhaps the only person you helped may realize it, but s/he may accept it as if s/he deserved it and not even be grateful.

Yet, what you do in secret is always recognized by the Lord, and it reveals your heart for Him. So, those of you working in secret for His kingdom, don't lose heart and keep going. You will certainly not lose your reward.

#keepgoing #noreligion #letyourlifeshine #notofthisworld #bedifferent #meaningfullife #loveconquersall

Sunday, August 11, 2013, New York, NY

413.

For the love of money is the root of all kinds of
evil. And some people, craving money, have
wandered from the true faith and pierced
themselves with many sorrows. But you,
Timothy, are a man of God; so run from all these
evil things. Pursue righteousness and a godly life,
along with faith, love, perseverance, and
gentleness. Fight the good fight for the true
faith. Hold tightly to the eternal life to which God
has called you, which you have confessed so
well before many witnesses.

1Timothy 6:10-12

Money is important, so are jobs or businesses we own. With them, we can advance the kingdom of God too! However, consider the loss if that ever becomes our priority even before God. A gentle reminder, we began our work and professions to serve God. Some of us committed our businesses from their inception to the Lord.

Our kingdom work in the marketplace must take second place to our relationship with God. It is the heart that God looks at, and our relationship with God is of utmost importance.

In our work, let us continually ask ourselves, Is Jesus my Lord? Is He more important to me than the riches of the work?

Make God your center, your number one priority. Let no idols steer us away.

#makegodpriority #relationshipsmatter #bethankful #trustgod #godisenough #turntogod #walkwithgod

Monday, August 12, 2013, New York, NY

2Timothy

414.

For God has not given us a spirit of fear and
timidity, but of power, love, and self-discipline.

Paul writes to Timothy again to encourage him. The church has basically beaten him up emotionally. Timothy may be feeling as if no one is following, no one cares, and people are criticizing him.

Christians who are passionate for the Lord often go through these training. These training is only reserved for the few through whom God plans to do great things.

Consider the lives of John the Baptist, the apostles, and even Jesus himself. As lovers of God, be grateful that you receive such treatment because you know God is with you. (Just one thing—as you go through these trials, check your heart and remain in Him)

Verse 7 says "for God has not given us a spirit of fear and timidity, but of power, love, and self-discipline."

Paul encourages us to not give up. Consider:

Fear = backing away. Stopping from what God leads us to do.

Timidity = to be shy.

Christians cannot be in fear or be shy, for we have a greater message we need to deliver.

Rather, let us consider these words for our lives:

Power = Know that God is with you in your speech and actions. He does the powerful work. Trust, for it is not about us.

Love = Even when others hurt you, you love them

Self-Discipline = do not fall into temptation because others hurt you. Do not hurt them back, do not lose the love of Jesus despite how cruel and mean others may be.

Stay strong! Especially those of you who are certain that God has an amazing and awesome plan for your life. (This is all of you!)

#gowhengodcalls #mygodissobig #comeholyspirit #godusesregularpeople #godisourstrength #trustgod
#obeygod

Tuesday, August 13, 2013, New York, NY

415.

Timothy, my dear son, be strong through the grace that God gives you in Christ Jesus.

2Timothy 2:1

We can be strong because of the grace of God.

Whenever we feel tired or lacking, we can simply go to God and ask, "give me strength" or "give me what i need." Because our God is gracious and loves us, He will supply all that we need. We lack nothing because he is our God.

#wehaveallthatweneed #hisgraceissufficient #remaininhislove #godprovides #godisfaithful #godisforus

Tuesday, February 11, 2020, Old Tappan, NJ USA

416.

> In a wealthy home some utensils are made of gold and silver, and some are made of wood and clay. The expensive utensils are used for special occasions, and the cheap ones are for everyday use. If you keep yourself pure, you will be a special utensil for honorable use. Your life will be clean, and you will be ready for the Master to use you for every good work.
>
> 2Timothy 2:20-21

We are all made unique and have unique destinies.

Verse 21 tells us to keep ourselves pure. That's what we are called to be in order to fulfill our ultimate destiny, which is the best path for our lives.

Pure = remaining in Christ, being purified because of what He has done, abiding in Him, and trusting Him as Lord of your life (see rest of verse 21).

Some of us may be concerned about our future. We may ask about what we would ever mount to. The truth is that God has made us unique with a unique purpose. Whatever that is, it would be something awesome and amazing. We know this because when God does things, it is often (always?) something huge in the big picture of things.

So then, trust that God is in control and do what we are called to—stay pure. Remain in Him.

#remaininhislove #notofthisworld #godisenough #favorwithgod #comeholyspirit #lifetransformation #noreligion

Wednesday, August 14, 2013, New York, NY

For people will love only themselves and their money. They will be boastful and proud, scoffing at God, disobedient to their parents, and ungrateful. They will consider nothing sacred. They will be unloving and unforgiving; they will slander others and have no self-control. They will be cruel and hate what is good. They will betray their friends, be reckless, be puffed up with pride, and love pleasure rather than God. They will act religious, but they will reject the power that could make them godly. Stay away from people like that! Yes, and everyone who wants to live a godly life in Christ Jesus will suffer persecution. But evil people and impostors will flourish. They will deceive others and will themselves be deceived. But you must remain faithful to the things you have been taught. You know they are true, for you know you can trust those who taught you. All Scripture is inspired by God and is useful to teach us what is true and to make us realize what is wrong in our lives. It corrects us when we are wrong and teaches us to do what is right. God uses it to prepare and equip his people to do every good work.

2Timothy 3:2-5,12-14,16-17

Many good messages here:

Verses 2-5. When I was in high school, I remember a Jehovah's Witnesses coming to my door and showing me this passage. They asked me if I felt this verse speaks truthfully about the world today. Though their version of the Bible had a different transliteration, the message was the same.

Yes, this is what we experience in the world today. I can point to capitalism, I can point to the economy, I can point to the brokenness—whatever it is, it leads to the results portrayed in this passage.

Even in the Church today, we are stuck in religion. We need the grace of God to break into our hearts and free us from these chains.

Thank God that He has provided a way for us through Jesus, His Son.

Verses 12-14. Believers will face persecution, and more so in our days within the churches. This is where we need to rely on God for His guidance. Especially, when we fight against religion, we too may become religious; that is, without love and have our hearts hardened as we may fight for which law or who is right.

Let us remain in humility, in love, and in power. Not shrinking back in our love for the people.

Verses 16-17. May God's people remain in the Word and remain steadfast in it. The Word is what centers us—the Word is God (see John 1).

#calling #loveothers #wearethechurch #relationshipsmatter #blessothers #loveconquersall #noreligion

Thursday, August 15, 2013, New York, NY

418.

> But you should keep a clear mind in every situation. Don't be afraid of suffering for the Lord. Work at telling others the Good News, and fully carry out the ministry God has given you.
>
> 2Timothy 4:5

God has given each of us a unique mission, a ministry, for our lives. Some of us are currently business owners, students, or employees; while at the same time, we are fathers, children, friends, lovers, etc.

God has placed you where you are with a purpose. Our goal is to remain in Him and trust Him as we "carry out the ministry."

How should we carry out the ministry God has given us? We need to do so with a clear mind.

In this world, there will be confusion as so many things are going on—but we must remain firmly rooted on the Word. When times come for decisions, ensure you are remaining in the Word.

At some occasions, prepare to suffer and experience difficulties as God leads you through it. Know that in the end, it will be for your benefit.

Read, meditate, walk as the Lord guides you through His Word.

#trustgod #comeholyspirit #visionary #godisfaithful #walkinfaith #pathsstraight #hisgraceissufficient

Friday, August 16, 2013, New York, NY

Titus

419.

> This letter is from Paul, a slave of God and an apostle of Jesus Christ. I have been sent to proclaim faith to those God has chosen and to teach them to know the truth that shows them how to live godly lives.
>
> Titus 1:1

In another letter from Paul, similar to his letter to Timothy, he lays out that we are to "live" lives worthy of being a Christian and talks about the position of Christian leaders.

As Christians, we are called to be the light for a dying nation. This calls us to aspire to growth and to lead others. God calls us to be leaders, whether we hold a title or not.

The question goes toward growth—for as many years as you have been a Christian, have you been growing? Has your life been transforming to the character mentioned in this chapter? Have you been conforming to His will?

Many leaders with titles often assume they have, and cause many difficulties for those who are trying to grow. As for us, regardless of titles or not, may we live blameless lives so that we would represent Jesus "through" our lives.

#letyourlifeshine #bedifferent #notofthisworld #meaningfullife #lookup #narrowpath #makegodpriority

Saturday, August 17, 2013, New York, NY

420.

> For the grace of God has been revealed,
> bringing salvation to all people. And we are
> instructed to turn from godless living and sinful
> pleasures. We should live in this evil world with
> wisdom, righteousness, and devotion to God,
> while we look forward with hope to that
> wonderful day when the glory of our great God
> and Savior, Jesus Christ, will be revealed. He
> gave his life to free us from every kind of sin, to
> cleanse us, and to make us his very own people,
> totally committed to doing good deeds.

Titus 2:11-14

Beautiful words.

1. Turn away (Repent)

2. Live (Demonstrate God through our lives)

3. Look forward with hope

4. Do good

May our lives represent the goodness of our God.

#letyourlifeshine #comeholyspirit #befruitful #wearethechurch #keepgoing #bedifferent #narrowpath

Sunday, August 18, 2013, New York, NY

421.

I am planning to send either Artemas or Tychicus to you. As soon as one of them arrives, do your best to meet me at Nicopolis, for I have decided to stay there for the winter. Do everything you can to help Zenas the lawyer and Apollos with their trip. See that they are given everything they need. Our people must learn to do good by meeting the urgent needs of others; then they will not be unproductive. Everybody here sends greetings. Please give my greetings to the believers - all who love us. May God's grace be with you all.

Titus 3:12-15

When I was in high school, I met Jesus and had such great zeal for the Lord as result. I wrote a letter to several churches in the area to encourage the pastors to keep going. (Funny when I think about it now, here's a little kid writing letters to adults). Though I have been commended by the pastors who received the letters, I definitely see a flaw in one part as I read today's passage.

I had written that we need to focus on the important stuff such the salvation by faith in Jesus Christ and living a life representing Him... and I downplayed verses such as verses 12-15 above. I stated that churches in today's times focus on irrelevant and less important things. Certainly, there were some truths to that, but I thought the verses above were not important portions of Scripture.

These verses point to fellowship, and support for other believers, which is so critical. Greeting one another, sharing the love of Jesus Christ!

I now realize living for Jesus is a team effort, not something one does on his/her own building up on self-disciplines and living a perfect, methodical life. It is about each other—to be toward one another. Let us remember one another in our prayers and trust God to develop an amazing fellowship amongst us.

#relationshipsmatter #bethereforoneanother #comeasyouare #blessothers #loveothers #wearethechurch

Monday, August 19, 2013, New York, NY

Philemon

422.

And to our sister Apphia, and to our fellow
soldier Archippus, and to the church that meets
in your house.

Philemon 1:2

Verse 2. "To the church that meets in your house."

Paul and Timothy writes this letter to the church that meets in a house.

Doesn't a church need a well-known name where we can post online, with an address where we can put in our bulletins?

Church is the people who love God.

Wherever they meet, whether that is in a house or a church building or at six flags or at a river rafting—this becomes the church. The house church is powerful because this is where we develop fellowship and honor God together in a small group. In these gatherings, we can see God move and do amazing things. You are the church—may your lives represent our Lord and King.

#lifetransformation #bethereforoneanother #wearethechurch #relationshipsmatter #noreligion

Tuesday, August 20, 2013, New York, NY

Hebrews

423.

> You will fold them up like a cloak and discard them like old clothing. But you are always the same; you will live forever."

Hebrews 1:12

Hebrews flows like a beautiful sermon.

It tells the greatness of Jesus and the vast importance of what He has done. Because of what He has done, we can now rest.

Today, I am drawn to verse 12. "But you are always the same; you will live forever."

In our lives, things are always shifting. Perhaps for some of us, each day is different, some of us, perhaps by month, year, phases, or seasons. We may work in a new environment, interact with people of different personalities, start something new, experience loss, or experience joy.

In all this, we would like stability, a changeless happiness with no surprises, and life is certainly not like that! Yet, our God has never changed—He always was, is, and will be. And that constant God is for us and will walk with us.

Hebrews   139

So in our current lives, He can certainly lead us to the best path. When we go through confusion in life, let us seek Him more and listen intently.

Ultimately, our hope is in life after our physical body passes away, the eternal life. He will take us home and we will be at rest.

#godisfaithful #godisable #godprovides #trustgod #listentogod #pathsstraight #remaininhislove #walkinfaith

Wednesday, August 21, 2013, New York, NY

424.

> Because God's children are human beings - made of flesh and blood - the Son also became flesh and blood. For only as a human being could he die, and only by dying could he break the power of the devil, who had the power of death.
>
> Hebrews 2:14

Jesus came to be like us.

It was so that He may know the sufferings we go through and lead us by experience of human living. That means, as we go through difficulties in our lives, we can trust that God is not speaking from afar without understanding us. He truly knows what we are going through, and despite that, He wants to lead us to the best. This is how God allows us to rest.

We don't need to worry about tomorrow, or what needs to be done in our lives.

One day at a time, trust and let God. Listen and follow. This is what is expected of people of faith.

#letgoletgod #trustgod #bedifferent #noreligion #listentogod #obeygod #gowhengodcalls #restwithgod

Thursday, August 22, 2013, New York, NY

425.

> So I was angry with them, and I said, 'Their hearts always turn away from me. They refuse to do what I tell them.' So in my anger I took an oath: 'They will never enter my place of rest.' Be careful then, dear brothers and sisters. Make sure that your own hearts are not evil and unbelieving, turning you away from the living God. You must warn each other every day, while it is still "today," so that none of you will be deceived by sin and hardened against God.

Hebrews 3:10-13

We read the story of Moses and wonder why these Israel people were so stubborn—when all they had to do was follow God! They were so close to making it to the promised land, and all of them, except two, failed to make it. "Stupid!" we would say.

Then, the question turns back to our lives… how about us?

We are in the same boat with the Holy Spirit leading us. All we have to do is follow Him! Now, only if we would only follow. (Do you see cyclical pattern here?)

This is indeed hard, and this is what the writer of Hebrews is exhorting us—to keep the faith and keep following in obedience.

Because it is hard, it is not meant to be done alone, but by encouraging one another to stay strong.

So today, center your life on God, and when ready, encourage a brother or sister in Christ to remain faithful to Him.

#betherefioroneanother #keepgoing #wearethechurch #listentogod #gowhengodcalls #obeygod #trustgod

Friday, August 23, 2013, New York, NY

426.

> God's promise of entering his rest still stands, so
> we ought to tremble with fear that some of you
> might fail to experience it. For this good news -
> that God has prepared this rest - has been
> announced to us just as it was to them. But it did
> them no good because they did not share the
> faith of those who listened to God.

Hebrews 4:1-2

It's amazing how many people believe they are Christians because they attend church. When they are asked what they believe, they do not know and cannot explain it.

In this age, the writer of Hebrews is reminding us, the rest that we all want so much is available to us. However, we should not be deceived as if we have attained it by the things that we do.

The question is not what you have done, but rather, it is about our faith. That is, do you believe in God and what He has done? Then do you respond to the Lord by entering into a relationship with Him (or does it not matter to you)?

All of us in this Scripture reading, may we enter into that rest by our faith in God.

#restwithgod #trustgod #hisgraceissufficient #abandonall #renewal #comeholyspirit #walkwithgod

Saturday, August 24, 2013, New York, NY

427.

> Even though Jesus was God's Son, he learned
> obedience from the things he suffered.

Hebrews 5:8

Praise God for your suffering.

When we suffer, we may get frustrated toward God and complain that He is not good. Well, He certainly is good, and good toward you. He loves you and wants you to go the best path for your life.

For those of us who believe in Him, we know it is important to obey (follow) His guidance—this guidance will come with suffering and difficulties—but we need to overcome that (trusting in God along the way) and press on.

It is through those suffering that we learn obedience and ultimately follow the best path for our lives.

So, stay strong and don't waiver in your faith through your difficulties. Refocus, recenter your life on Him, and keep walking in faith.

#walkinfaith #noworries #trustgod #bethankful #listentogod #submittogod #godisfaithful

Sunday, August 25, 2013, New York, NY

428.

Then you will not become spiritually dull and indifferent. Instead, you will follow the example of those who are going to inherit God's promises because of their faith and endurance.

Hebrews 6:12

As we live in obedience to the Lord, we may find ourselves in a greater mess. These are times when we question, have I been obedient? Is the Lord truly with me? Is He really there? should I stop and turn back to my comfortable life? Don't.

God's promises for you have not changed. Example of those that turned back are the Israelites when their faith wavered throughout their times in the desert and even when they were very close to the Promised Land.

Examples of those who kept their faith (New Living Translation calls them "Great Examples of Faith" or I call them Heroes of Faith—See Heb 11, coming soon) include people like Joseph who became second highest ruler of a large kingdom starting from position of a slave.

This chapter begins to speak of Abraham. If you consider Abraham's life, he had to give up everything he owned to follow God's command to go to a land that He will show him. This was a land that Abraham hasn't even seen yet! and God was demanding that he leaves everything and go. Through his journey, he felt his life was threatened, so he had to lie his way out. When we too face circumstances like this, we often want to give up and turn back. Consider the rewards Abraham has received—just as Google, Facebook, and Apple changed the way the world does things, Abraham's action led to a revolutionary change for the people of Israel.

We too are part of God's plans, and He has an amazing, wonderful, and awesome things laid out for us. So, when you recognize the promises of God, and He calls you to obey, do it in full faith. As we go along, when we get discouraged, don't waver in your faith. Believe, trust—and keep going in full endurance. Stay strong!

#gowhengodcalls #calling #walkinfaith #wehaveallthatweneed #befruitful #makegodpriority #mygodissobig

Monday, August 26, 2013, New York, NY

> This Melchizedek was king of the city of Salem and also a priest of God Most High. When Abraham was returning home after winning a great battle against the kings, Melchizedek met him and blessed him. Then Abraham took a tenth of all he had captured in battle and gave it to Melchizedek. The name Melchizedek means "king of justice," and king of Salem means "king of peace."
>
> Hebrews 7:1-2

These two verses expound on a very important topic—what our roles are as congregants and what the roles of the pastors are.

Abraham came back from his professional duties—to us, this may be our being a student, a business owner, engineer, manager, or a housewife—Melchizedek came to meet and blessed Abraham.

The roles of pastors are to bless God's people to faithfully commit and do well on the tasks God has given them.

Here, we can quell the religious act of "going all out for God, and so, I'll become a pastor" syndrome. Not all people are called to be pastors. It is a special calling from God, where when one is not called, s/he should not go toward that role, but rather consider serving God where s/he is and ask God for further clarification. God has amazing plans for each of us and it never requires us to be religious. He calls each of us into a relationship with Him.

Abraham gave tenth (a portion) of his earnings to the priest (to give to the Lord, as the priest is to represent giving to God). It is important as believers to acknowledge our fruits come from God. Tithing, giving a tenth, is a figure, to which we ought to give as a minimum while planning to give more as our hearts lead us. It is acknowledging and letting go of what we may believe to be most important and leave it at God's hands.

So be faithful in what you do; don't seek religion, but a relationship. Acknowledge Him in all you do, and let go of anything before God that may become more important to you than who He is.

#noreligion #makegodpriority #noworries #letyourlifeshine #befruitful #trustgod #wearethechurch

Tuesday, August 27, 2013, New York, NY

430.

> They serve in a system of worship that is only a copy, a shadow of the real one in heaven. For when Moses was getting ready to build the Tabernacle, God gave him this warning: "Be sure that you make everything according to the pattern I have shown you here on the mountain."
>
> Hebrews 8:5

Whatever walk you may be going through in life, we can be certain of the real-that-we-will-see that is in heaven.

We live in an imperfect world where there are many faults (see verse 7), and we will certainly experience difficulties, sadness, gloom, troubles. Yet, there is the fullness of life waiting for us in heaven. So, do not despair, but look up to the Lord who will guide you even in this confusing, fast-paced world. He will certainly not let us go.

#trustgod #hisgraceissufficient #renewal #letgoletgod #keepgoing #letyourlifeshine #noworries #meaningfullife

Wednesday, August 28, 2013, New York, NY

431.

> By these regulations the Holy Spirit revealed that
> the entrance to the Most Holy Place was not
> freely open as long as the Tabernacle and the
> system it represented were still in use. That is
> why he is the one who mediates a new covenant
> between God and people, so that all who are
> called can receive the eternal inheritance God
> has promised them. For Christ died to set them
> free from the penalty of the sins they had
> committed under that first covenant. so also
> Christ died once for all time as a sacrifice to take
> away the sins of many people. He will come
> again, not to deal with our sins, but to bring
> salvation to all who are eagerly waiting for him.

Hebrews 9:8,15,28

Direct access to God.

That's what we have as a result of what Jesus has done. And, we don't have to worry about if we sacrificed enough, missed any sins for which we need to atone. We can rest knowing that we are fully forgiven and accepted just as we are. Only condition is for us to accept Jesus as our Lord.

For those of us who have, when Jesus comes back, it will not be for a judgment (where we would need to worry), but rather salvation. It will mean freedom from our worries, fears, difficulties, lacks, and sickness—and simply joy, acceptance, passion, and love.

#godlovesus #godisfaithful #hisgraceissufficient #bethankful #weareforgivenandfree

Thursday, August 29, 2013, New York, NY

If they could have provided perfect cleansing,
the sacrifices would have stopped, for the
worshipers would have been purified once for all
time, and their feelings of guilt would have
disappeared. But instead, those sacrifices
actually reminded them of their sins year after
year. And when sins have been forgiven, there is
no need to offer any more sacrifices. So do not
throw away this confident trust in the Lord.
Remember the great reward it brings you!
Patient endurance is what you need now, so that
you will continue to do God's will. Then you will
receive all that he has promised.

Hebrews 10:2-3,18,35-36

Verses 2-3. Some of us may be thinking about the mistakes we made this week, perhaps even yesterday, and we may continue to mull over these things. With all the self-help materials out there, and how the world tells us we must be better, we keep striving and striving, thinking about how much of a failure we are. In the end, just burn out.

Let me tell you of the Good News of Jesus. Because of what Jesus has done, we no longer need to allow guilt and regrets to take over our mind. Scriptures tell us that Jesus has taken care of all our sins once and for all, and we no longer need to make sacrifices. We can rest in His loving arms. Sure, we'll make mistakes; and sure, we will fail to meet expectations; but guess what, it doesn't matter.

What is important is our faith in Jesus, that is, our trust, our relationship, our walk with Him, and our obedience to His guidance.

So, don't give up on your journey. Ask Jesus to pick you up from where you are, and commit to follow Him.

#walkwithgod #trustgod #obeygod #keepgoing #letyourlifeshine #bedifferent #meaningfullife #bethankful

Friday, August 30, 2013, New York, NY

433.

> Faith is the confidence that what we hope for will actually happen; it gives us assurance about things we cannot see. quenched the flames of fire, and escaped death by the edge of the sword. Their weakness was turned to strength. They became strong in battle and put whole armies to flight. Women received their loved ones back again from death. But others were tortured, refusing to turn from God in order to be set free. They placed their hope in a better life after the resurrection. Some were jeered at, and their backs were cut open with whips. Others were chained in prisons. Some died by stoning, some were sawed in half, and others were killed with the sword. Some went about wearing skins of sheep and goats, destitute and oppressed and mistreated. They were too good for this world, wandering over deserts and mountains, hiding in caves and holes in the ground. All these people earned a good reputation because of their faith, yet none of them received all that God had promised. For God had something better in mind for us, so that they would not reach perfection without us.

> Hebrews 11:1,34-40

And now, here is the famous chapter on faith.

Verse 1. Simplifying the word faith, it means to trust. Utmost, in all our circumstances, are we able to trust God that He would protect us, guide us, lead us, be with us? This is the crux of faith. It is by trust that all heroes of faith persevered and earned their reputation.

Faith may be better defined as believing in the promises of God. When we start a business or set out to do something great—there will certainly be roadblocks or difficulties along the way. Now, this is where our trust in God may waver. What if this fails, what if God doesn't sustain me, what if I cannot get the cash flow to cover me for the next few months? As the Lord has guided you to start something, our faith would allow us to trust that God will see it through until the end. Holding on to that promise would enable us to keep trusting and not be discouraged

Verse 34. "Their weakness was turned to strength. They became strong in battle and put whole armies to flight." By faith God can make the impossible happen. Trust, because He's got it all under control.

Verses 35-40. Oooh... so, here's what trust looks like. Not everything will be perfect in the world's standards. Some of us may die or "fail" in world's eyes because of our faith. It is because that perfection is not here yet.

Certainly, God can use you to build a perfect business where your earnings can support the Church and advance His kingdom; but for some of us, that journey of starting the business may be here, but the fulfillment of the promise may come beyond our time here. (Stay tuned for next chapter).

Ultimately, God calls us to a relationship, and this is of utmost importance—can you trust Him? do you believe He is good? good to you, good for you, and will lead you to a good path?

Then our automatic response is, "yes Lord" and we would follow (definition of being obedient).

Don't waver in your faith. In your current occupation, keep on believing in His promises. Stay strong!

#keepgoing #trustgod #breakthrough #hisgraceissufficient #remaininhislove #letgoletgod #calling #visionary

Saturday, August 31, 2013, New York, NY

434.

> All these people died still believing what God had promised them. They did not receive what was promised, but they saw it all from a distance and welcomed it. They agreed that they were foreigners and nomads here on earth.

Hebrews 11:13

God's calling goes beyond even our own lives. It is something much greater. He would lead us to accomplish something that great... the question remains... would we too, like the people of faith, go as He leads, or will we settle for comfort?

#letmywordsbefew #lifetransformation #makegodpriority #noreligion #walkinfaith #hisgraceissufficient

Friday, February 28, 2020, New York, NY USA

435.

> For our earthly fathers disciplined us for a few years, doing the best they knew how. But God's discipline is always good for us, so that we might share in his holiness. No discipline is enjoyable while it is happening - it's painful! But afterward there will be a peaceful harvest of right living for those who are trained in this way. For our God is a devouring fire.

Hebrews 12:10-11,29

Only those who receive training/discipline from God are able to make it in heaven. All things that can shaken out of us would be removed so that all that remain would be permanent and good.

#godhasaplan #godisfaithful #sovereigngod #favorwithgod #renewal #hisgraceissufficient #remaininhislove

Saturday, February 29, 2020, Old Tappan, NJ USA

436.

> Work at living in peace with everyone, and work at living a holy life, for those who are not holy will not see the Lord. Look after each other so that none of you fails to receive the grace of God. Watch out that no poisonous root of bitterness grows up to trouble you, corrupting many.

Hebrews 12:14-15

This chapter is full of gems. God loves us as His children, so be grateful to be called His, even through our times of discipline. Do not fail to listen in those times.

Verses 14-15 tells us about community. First set is directed at us

1. Work at live at peace with everyone (not that it will be possible with everyone)

2. Work on yourself—to live a holy life (be in constant relationship with God, trust and acknowledge God in all you do, do not lean on your own understanding)

3. Look after each other so they don't miss out—help them to stay focused on living a holy life

4. Watch for poisonous roots of bitterness, both amongst you and others. When you start getting frustrated with someone and bitterness begins to pile up, ask God to remove that, because Satan will use that to "corrupt many."

In the end, this community, or we, form the church of Jesus.

Let us remain faithful. When we see others falling astray, let's gently nudge others back to holiness.

#loveothers #blessothers #relationshipsmatter #letyourlifeshine #noreligion #wearethechurch #renewal

Sunday, September 1, 2013, New York, NY

437.

> Don't forget to show hospitality to strangers, for some who have done this have entertained angels without realizing it!

Hebrews 13:2

Let's continue to invite people to our home.

The act of inviting people to our home is a way we can serve others. When we go to another person's home, we have to ask for simple things like water because we do not know where it is. Since it is our house, our room, our kitchen, we know where things are and we can offer them good things like food.

Let others share in the blessings God has given us, and as the writer of Hebrews says, we are entertaining angels and our God by our love.

#blessothers #givetoothers #visionary #calling #relationshipsmatter #loveconquersall #wearethechurch

Sunday, March 1, 2020, Ridgefield, NJ USA

James

438.

> If you need wisdom, ask our generous God, and
> he will give it to you. He will not rebuke you for
> asking. But when you ask him, be sure that your
> faith is in God alone. Do not waver, for a person
> with divided loyalty is as unsettled as a wave of
> the sea that is blown and tossed by the wind. So
> get rid of all the filth and evil in your lives, and
> humbly accept the word God has planted in your
> hearts, for it has the power to save your souls.

> James 1:5-6,21

Trust in the Lord. He will guide you to the best path for your life!

Living in the world where we are told we need morel: better fitness, better education, better job, or more money, it is easy to get confused and wonder exactly what would be the best for our lives. The Good News tells us that He will lead us to what is the best for us.

Verses 5-6. Let your trust be in the Lord, and not others, not what the world says, and not even yourself. Trust in Him. This can only happen when you have a relationship with God.

Verse 21. Let go, and let God. Only by doing so, He can lead you to the best path for your life.

#letgoletgod #pathsstraight #lookup #bedifferent #notofthisworld #noworries #hisgraceissufficient

Tuesday, September 3, 2013, New York, NY

439.

> My dear brothers and sisters, how can you claim
> to have faith in our glorious Lord Jesus Christ if
> you favor some people over others? For
> example, suppose someone comes into your
> meeting dressed in fancy clothes and expensive
> jewelry, and another comes in who is poor and
> dressed in dirty clothes.

James 2:1-2

Call to not be selfish.

The example James provides points to how we may care for others only when they may be a benefit to us. When we show favoritism toward others, it is not pure agape love, the love that comes from God, rather, it would be self-serving acting (fake love).

We can love everyone when we are confident that God cares for us. Only people who believe they need to be in control would pretend to love for their selfish purposes.

When we know we are loved by God and that He will take care of all our needs, we can freely love others with the love of Jesus.

#bethankful #trustgod #godisfaithful #godprovides #godlovesus #godisforus #waitongod #expectfromgod

Tuesday, March 3, 2020, New York, NY USA

440.

> So whatever you say or whatever you do,
> remember that you will be judged by the law
> that sets you free. There will be no mercy for
> those who have not shown mercy to others. But
> if you have been merciful, God will be merciful
> when he judges you.

James 2:12-13

The law says do this, do that, don't do this, don't do that.

That is not the law Christians live by. We live under grace. As we have been forgiven, we can freely forgive others. As our wrongs have been tolerated, we can tolerate others' wrongdoing.

Don't be afraid of what others impose on you. We live under freedom, and we live under the Spirit's guidance.

Trust Him and move forward without fears in life. Remain in Him.

#nofear #loveconquersall #noreligion #letyourlifeshine #noworries #remaininhislove #weareforgivenandfree

Wednesday, September 4, 2013, New York, NY

441.

> So humble yourselves before God. Resist the
> devil, and he will flee from you. Come close to
> God, and God will come close to you. Wash your
> hands, you sinners; purify your hearts, for your
> loyalty is divided between God and the world.

James 4:7-8

It's about the heart.

Book of James is full of practical experiences of life. This chapter in particular talks about fights, jealousy, judging others, and even pride/self-confidence.

All that—he declares—is how Satan is pulling us toward his ways. Our relentless response would be to cling to God, trust Him, and remain in Him (relentlessly fight for your relationship with God).

So, humble yourselves, resist the devil, and come close to God.

Stay strong everyone! May the Lord grant you peace.

#lookup #trustgod #walkinfaith #heartmatters #comeholyspirit #godisourstrength #godprovides #godisfaithful

Friday, September 6, 2013, New York, NY

442.

> Are any of you suffering hardships? You should pray. Are any of you happy? You should sing praises. Are any of you sick? You should call for the elders of the church to come and pray over you, anointing you with oil in the name of the Lord. Such a prayer offered in faith will heal the sick, and the Lord will make you well. And if you have committed any sins, you will be forgiven. Confess your sins to each other and pray for each other so that you may be healed. The earnest prayer of a righteous person has great power and produces wonderful results.
>
> James 5:13-16

Power of Prayer.

Prayer has the ability to heal you—emotionally, physically, and even in your circumstances. Don't ever give up on your prayers, both for yourself and for others. It is through prayer that God's power is revealed.

In order to find effective results of prayer, remain in the Lord—be right toward God and others—and your prayers will be a benefit to others.

This is how we can let others know about God—by remaining in Him and blessing others through prayer.

Join us for prayer tents as we pray for others and reveal the power of God.

#godprovides #godisable #godisenough #blessingsfromgod #expectfromgod #favorwithgod #blessothers

Saturday, September 7, 2013, New York, NY

1Peter

443.

So think clearly and exercise self-control. Look forward to the gracious salvation that will come to you when Jesus Christ is revealed to the world. So you must live as God's obedient children. Don't slip back into your old ways of living to satisfy your own desires. You did not know any better then. But now you must be holy in everything you do, just as God who chose you is holy.

1Peter 1:13-15

Be different, because our God is different.

Holy means to be set apart or different. The call is to live lives that are different than that of people who do not believe in Jesus.

In what ways should we be different? In how we live, and specifically in how we control ourselves (self-control). After believing in Jesus, our pursuits and desires are changed. Instead of living for ourselves, we want to live for God and others. The call is to not slip back to our old way of selfish living.

May all that is important to us be dedicated to/submitted before Him.

#bedifferent #abandonall #letyourlifeshine #notofthisworld #narrowpath #comeholyspirit #submittogod

Saturday, March 7, 2020, Closter, NJ USA

444.

> You who are slaves must accept the authority of your masters with all respect. Do what they tell you - not only if they are kind and reasonable, but even if they are cruel. For God is pleased with you when you do what you know is right and patiently endure unfair treatment. Of course, you get no credit for being patient if you are beaten for doing wrong. But if you suffer for doing good and endure it patiently, God is pleased with you.
>
> 1Peter 2:18-20

At work, school, church, or wherever we may be, let us take the role of a servant as Jesus demonstrated in His life.

Trust God for the work we do. Love our bosses, superiors and endure even if they do wrong to us.

We believe that God is in control in all that we do.

#trustgod #honorgod #bedifferent #notofthisworld #lookup #pray #godisenough #godprovides #walkwithgod

Sunday, March 8, 2020, Old Tappan, NJ USA

445.

> Finally, all of you should be of one mind. Sympathize with each other. Love each other as brothers and sisters. Be tenderhearted, and keep a humble attitude. Don't repay evil for evil. Don't retaliate with insults when people insult you. Instead, pay them back with a blessing. That is what God has called you to do, and he will bless you for it. Instead, you must worship Christ as Lord of your life. And if someone asks about your Christian hope, always be ready to explain it.

> 1Peter 3:8-9,15

Peter expounds about our being toward one another in this chapter.

To wives, to husbands, to believers, and even to those who persecute you. Despite how others may be toward us, we will keep our eyes on the prize and worship God, and in turn, love even those who hurt us.

I see this as salvation. Many (all?) of us cannot have a positive attitude toward those who hurt us, and as our attitude grows negative, and we suffer. We grow in bitterness, anger, narrow-minded thinking, and we simply sink into depravity, depression, and frustration. We no longer live out the joy that God has in store for us.

Yet, salvation comes by no other name than by Jesus. By our faith and trust in Him, he can transform our hearts so that we may love others and even love God when our hearts are unwilling (Ezekiel 36:26-27).

This enables us to truly "live" despite our circumstances, be thankful, and be in joy.

Consider in your life what you may need to let go and leave with God. Cast your burdens on Him for He cares for you. He has the ability to transform your hearts and your thinking for your good.

#lifetransformation #bethankful #nothingisimpossiblewithgod #lookup #notofthisworld #godprovides

Tuesday, September 10, 2013, New York, NY

446.

> You won't spend the rest of your lives chasing your own desires, but you will be anxious to do the will of God.
>
> 1Peter 4:2

May this be how God transforms our hearts.

Instead of seeking our own pursuits, may our goals be in line with what God has in store for us—the best for our lives!

In the best path, we will certainly face difficulties (and Satan will cast many doubts to make us feel as if we are not going the best way and to turn us back to the life of selfishness and living for ourselves. Yet, Peter tells us to endure (verses 12-19).

Let us keep doing what is right as the Holy Spirit leads us!

Stay strong my brothers and sisters—God is going to do some amazing things!

#trustgod #favorwithgod #godcorrects #godprovides #godisourstrength #comeholyspirit #lookup

Wednesday, September 11, 2013, New York, NY

447.

> Most important of all, continue to show deep love for each other, for love covers a multitude of sins. Cheerfully share your home with those who need a meal or a place to stay. God has given each of you a gift from his great variety of spiritual gifts. Use them well to serve one another. Do you have the gift of speaking? Then speak as though God himself were speaking through you. Do you have the gift of helping others? Do it with all the strength and energy that God supplies. Then everything you do will bring glory to God through Jesus Christ. All glory and power to him forever and ever! Amen.

1Peter 4:8-11

Let us serve one another with what God has given us.

If we have a home, we should invite people to welcome and feed them.

If we have things, we should share it with those who may need it.

If we have talents, we should use it to help/support others.

All that God has given us is to fulfill verse 8, which is to love one another, which is truly how we love God.

#blessothers #givetoothers #loveothers #bemerciful #relationshipsmatter #befruitful #wearethechurch

Tuesday, March 10, 2020, New York, NY USA

2Peter

448.

> By his divine power, God has given us
> everything we need for living a godly life. We
> have received all of this by coming to know him,
> the one who called us to himself by means of his
> marvelous glory and excellence. And because of
> his glory and excellence, he has given us great
> and precious promises. These are the promises
> that enable you to share his divine nature and
> escape the world's corruption caused by human
> desires. In view of all this, make every effort to
> respond to God's promises. Supplement your
> faith with a generous provision of moral
> excellence, and moral excellence with
> knowledge, and knowledge with self-control, and
> self-control with patient endurance, and patient
> endurance with godliness, and godliness with
> brotherly affection, and brotherly affection with
> love for everyone.

2Peter 1:3-7

His promise—the source of our joy in every circumstance.

His promise enables us to share in his divine nature and escape from the fallacies (the struggles, the pain, and the hurts) of this world.

That promise is that he would walk with us and transform our hearts of stone to fluidity.

Regardless of what you may be going through, cling to the promise of God, that He is leading you to the best and lean on Him. As you do, may you see the transformation in your life that grows into faith, moral excellence, knowledge, self-control, patience, godliness, and love.

#heartmatters #lifetransformation #breakthrough #renewal #calling #remaininhislove #befruitful #lookup

Friday, September 13, 2013, New York, NY

1John

449.

> But if we are living in the light, as God is in the light, then we have fellowship with each other, and the blood of Jesus, his Son, cleanses us from all sin.

1John 1:7

True Fellowship of Believers.

In the church, fellowship is encouraged, and in fact, we even have cell groups in the church that are designed for recurring gatherings. Many of us may feel that gathering in itself is the point, and as meetings become less helpful to us, we may frown upon meeting together.

True Christian fellowship is about centering on Christ ("living in the light"). Only when we are centered on Him, the fellowship comes alive: we get healed, our lives' circumstances are restored, and we find peace.

Fellowships can also be an opportunity to welcome new members, but we as believers must hold to our center—our relationship with Jesus Christ.

So, brothers and sisters, as we live through the week, even to the day when we get together in a meeting, let us remain strong in Him and encourage one another (or be encouraged by one another) as we get together.

Be relentless in keeping your relationship with the Lord.

#makegodpriority #remaininhislove #wearethechurch #hisgraceissufficient #blessothers #bethereforoneanother

Monday, September 16, 2013, New York, NY

450.

> I am writing to you who are God's children because your sins have been forgiven through Jesus. I am writing to you who are mature in the faith because you know Christ, who existed from the beginning. I am writing to you who are young in the faith because you have won your battle with the evil one. I have written to you who are God's children because you know the Father. I have written to you who are mature in the faith because you know Christ, who existed from the beginning. I have written to you who are young in the faith because you are strong. God's word lives in your hearts, and you have won your battle with the evil one.
>
> 1John 2:12-14

Keeping the fire.

What's interesting in the verses above talks about three circumstances / positions / timelines of life.

To God's children—all Christians—you are forgiven through Jesus Christ and you know the Father. For the original readers of this letter, it is to serve as a reminder that we have a relationship with God because of what Jesus has done. As believers, we shall never forget this basic truth. Without his intervention, we would have no access to God. It is because of His grace that we can commune with God.

To those who are mature in faith, or to long-time believers, you know Christ, who existed from the beginning. The warning here is to those who have believed for a long time. It is a call to not lose the fire, as you know Jesus that has always been there with you! Don't lose faith. Don't go into religion mode. Don't let go of your relationship with God!

John recognizes that as time goes, we may begin to wander, especially as we go through life circumstances, struggles, and despair. Don't give up.

Finally, there's an address to those who are young in faith. Those of you who have just come into an intimate relationship with God, you have overcome the battle with the evil one.

Do you see why it is so important that people come to know the Lord? That is 90% of the battle to be in an intimate relationship with God. You really cannot be shaken from this faith once you've experienced it. God will hold you, and even as you waver, He will bring you back. And the faith of such young believers—amazing! They have tasted God, and are relentless in staying close with the Lord (because it's so good), and their actions are to do His will.

They are strong, as they have overcome the battle of the heart against the evil one.

Those of you who have never tasted this wonderful relationship with Christ, come to know Him. Only He can transform you. For those of you who have, don't lose the fire—let it be like those who are young in faith, your first love.

#godrestores #rightwithgod #godlovesus #godprovides #godisforus #abandonall #renewal
#lifetransformation

Tuesday, September 17, 2013, New York, NY

451.

Dear children, let's not merely say that we love each other; let us show the truth by our actions. Our actions will show that we belong to the truth, so we will be confident when we stand before God. Even if we feel guilty, God is greater than our feelings, and he knows everything. Dear friends, if we don't feel guilty, we can come to God with bold confidence. And we will receive from him whatever we ask because we obey him and do the things that please him. And this is his commandment: We must believe in the name of his Son, Jesus Christ, and love one another, just as he commanded us. Those who obey God's commandments remain in fellowship with him, and he with them. And we know he lives in us because the Spirit he gave us lives in us.

1John 3:18-24

God can set our heart at rest Some of us may be going through storms in life wondering when we can ever be at rest.

Our God promises rest. Don't let your hearts deceive you, for He is greater than our feelings and He knows everything. Live with trust in God, and let that spur on to love towards others.

When people criticize us, hurt us, or speak badly of us, don't let your heart be shaken and continue to trust in God. We can come to Him with bold confidence, as our lives are in one accord with Him.

Remain in fellowship with Him, as that is all that we need.

You're all I want, You're all I've ever needed, You're all I want, help me know You are near. (Lyrics from Draw me close to you).

#wehaveallthatweneed #hisgraceissufficient #restwithgod #waitongod #expectfromgod #godprovides

Wednesday, September 18, 2013, New York, NY

452.

> But you belong to God, my dear children. You have already won a victory over those people, because the Spirit who lives in you is greater than the spirit who lives in the world. Those people belong to this world, so they speak from the world's viewpoint, and the world listens to them. But we belong to God, and those who know God listen to us. If they do not belong to God, they do not listen to us. That is how we know if someone has the Spirit of truth or the spirit of deception.

1John 4:4-6

Difficult bosses, colleagues, people.

We have the Spirit of Christ and we belong to God. So just let it go: their incessant arguing, bullying, manipulation, and the ways they hurt you.

We have already won a victory over such people. Don't fall into the trap of emulating what they do, but trust God and smile. God's got it under control.

#letgoletgod #trustgod #lookup #narrowpath #loveconquersall #nofear #honorgod #bethankful #blessothers

Thursday, September 19, 2013, New York, NY

453.

> Everyone who believes that Jesus is the Christ
> has become a child of God. And everyone who
> loves the Father loves his children, too. We know
> we love God's children if we love God and obey
> his commandments. Loving God means keeping
> his commandments, and his commandments are
> not burdensome. For every child of God defeats
> this evil world, and we achieve this victory
> through our faith. And who can win this battle
> against the world? Only those who believe that
> Jesus is the Son of God. And we know that the
> Son of God has come, and he has given us
> understanding so that we can know the true
> God. And now we live in fellowship with the true
> God because we live in fellowship with his Son,
> Jesus Christ. He is the only true God, and he is
> eternal life. Dear children, keep away from
> anything that might take God's place in your
> hearts.

1John 5:1-5,20-21

Fellowship with others center on God.

Powerful set of verses. Everyone who loves God loves one another (v. 1). We love one another by loving God, which is to obey His commands. This in turn means we cannot love others without knowing God's commands and being obedient to Him. We love others by being on a solid relationship with God! How relieving this is! It means we do not have to be people-pleasers or always be nice to meet people's incessant demands. Our love for others is defined by our love for God! Not by what others think of us, not by how people believe we should have acted, done, or said.

We achieve victory through our faith in Jesus, because we love Him (v. 4-5).

And now that Jesus has given us a path to direct fellowship with God (v. 20), be relentless in protecting this relationship. Don't let anything, even your emotions or doubts, get in the way of trusting God in your hearts (v. 21).

#lovegod #rightwithgod #godlovesus #godisforus #godisenough #noreligion #relationshipsmatter

Friday, September 20, 2013, New York, NY

454.

> For every child of God defeats this evil world, and we achieve this victory through our faith. And who can win this battle against the world? Only those who believe that Jesus is the Son of God. We know that God's children do not make a practice of sinning, for God's Son holds them securely, and the evil one cannot touch them. Dear children, keep away from anything that might take God's place in your hearts.
>
> 1John 5:4-5,18,21

We overcome the world (and sin) by our faith and trust in Jesus. Let's not allow anything to take higher priority in our hearts than God.

#makegodpriority #noreligion #wearethechurch #abandonall #wehaveallthatweneed #pathsstraight

Thursday, March 19, 2020, New York, NY USA

2John

455.

Love means doing what God has commanded
us, and he has commanded us to love one
another, just as you heard from the beginning. I
have much more to say to you, but I don't want
to do it with paper and ink. For I hope to visit
you soon and talk with you face to face. Then
our joy will be complete.

2John 1:6,12

True love is obedience to God (v. 6). Following on from yesterday's message, John's second letter expounds that the depth of our love relationship with God is how we love one another.

Be relentless in sustaining your relationship with God. Remain in Him.

Verse 12. In the current technology age, many of us communicate away from each other. The technology, though it has its uses, corrodes communion and fellowship amongst believers. As believers, we have to also fight our busy task-driven lives to be with one another. That is what the church is, collective of believers of God.

#obeygod #lovegod #remaininhislove #noreligion #blessothers #loveothers #lifetransformation #beavailable

Saturday, September 21, 2013, New York, NY

456.

> I have much more to say to you, but I don't want to do it with paper and ink. For I hope to visit you soon and talk with you face to face. Then our joy will be complete.

2John 1:12

A person who has a relationship with God has desire to meet with other believers and have fellowship (relationship) with them.

This is unlike our modern day trend of text/emails/phone calls/facebook posts/linkedin messages that is only virtual and often impersonal.

Relationships occur because of time spent together, and that is what it means to be a disciple, to live out our lives together.

#onefamily #loveothers #blessothers #relationshipsmatter #beavailable #comeholyspirit #walkwithgod

Friday, March 20, 2020, New York, NY USA

3John

457.

> This letter is from John, the elder. I am writing to Gaius, my dear friend, whom I love in the truth.

John the elder.

Because of the abuses within the church of those who hold this title, the word elder sounds like a title of weakness. However, being an elder signifies that the person has a great, long-enduring, deeply-grown relationship with God.

In this world, people seek greater titles, and we can even see the churches rewarding people without the proper qualifications to keep their organization running.

As believers, let us not seek after titles in the church to have a "greater say" in matters, but let it be guided by our hearts. Go after a relentless relationship with our God, our Lord, our Father, and our Savior. From the depth of that relationship, may we spur unto one another and live a fruitful life led by the Spirit.

You are all called to do amazing things through your lives—fulfill it by trusting and being obedient to the Lord.

#listentogod #obeygod #calling #meaningfullife #lifetransformation #walkwithgod #pathsstraight #renewal

Sunday, September 22, 2013, New York, NY

Jude

458.

> But you, dear friends, must build each other up in your most holy faith, pray in the power of the Holy Spirit, and await the mercy of our Lord Jesus Christ, who will bring you eternal life. In this way, you will keep yourselves safe in God's love. And you must show mercy to those whose faith is wavering. Rescue others by snatching them from the flames of judgment. Show mercy to still others, but do so with great caution, hating the sins that contaminate their lives.
>
> Jude 1:20-23

But you, build each other up and be merciful.

Letter from Jude is short and to the point. There are people in the church who do whatever they want, and claim that their lifestyle is what it means to be a Christian. Such people disrupt the unity in the church and prevent people from coming to know the Lord.

For those of us who know the Lord, we have no need to brag or speak loudly because in our hearts, we are safe and secure in our relationship with our Father who leads us and protects us. Ask the Lord for peace in your heart if you are going through performance anxiety.

And as people who are saved, let us learn to hate sin, but love the people. This means we need to be able to distinguish what is sin as well. Let us delve into Scriptures and ask the Lord to teach us, to transform our understanding, and to break our rebellious hearts so that we may have fluidity of heart that follows as the Lord guides us.

#blessothers #relationshipsmatter #remaininhislove #noreligion #letyourlifeshine #wehaveallthatweneed

Monday, September 23, 2013, New York, NY

Revelation

459.

> "I know all the things you do. I have seen your
> hard work and your patient endurance. I know
> you don't tolerate evil people. You have
> examined the claims of those who say they are
> apostles but are not. You have discovered they
> are liars. You have patiently suffered for me
> without quitting. "But I have this complaint
> against you. You don't love me or each other as
> you did at first! Look how far you have fallen!
> Turn back to me and do the works you did at
> first. If you don't repent, I will come and remove
> your lampstand from its place among the
> churches.

Revelation 2:2-5

Come back!

This chapter and the next talks about how we, as the church collectively, can easily fall away from God's desire for a relationship. Each can be examined carefully to expose our hearts and show us how we can turn back to the Lord.

For today, I focus on the writing that was made to the first church, Ephesus. This is a church with a very good track record. They have held their services without fail, they know the Scriptures very well, and they DO things right.

What's the problem then? They don't have a relationship with God. Actually, they began with such a fervor like many of us do, but eventually they sank into religiousness.

They began to DO things and felt they were right with God as long as they kept doing what they were doing. We can never forget that God's original (and even today's) intent has always been to be in a relationship with His people, the church (or us, collectively).

Our activities cannot replace our direct relationship with God, which Jesus has purchased for us through the cross. This is why the call for us is "You don't love me or each other as you did at first! Look how far you have fallen! ... Turn back to me and do the works you did at first."

What did we do first when we believed in the Lord? I recall diving into Scriptures, spending time in reflection, prayer, singing praises, and sharing God with others. It's a heart-matter! Our hearts may have become too hardened from our everyday doing (including our busyness). Let's ask the Lord the soften our hearts so that we may receive Him and commune with Him once more.

"And I will give you a new heart, and I will put a new spirit in you. I will take out your stony, stubborn heart and give you a tender, responsive heart." Ezekiel 36:26

#turntogod #lovegod #heartmatters #abandonall #remaininhislove #noreligion #narrowpath #makegodpriority

Wednesday, September 25, 2013, New York, NY

460.

> "Yet there are some in the church in Sardis who have not soiled their clothes with evil. They will walk with me in white, for they are worthy. All who are victorious will be clothed in white. I will never erase their names from the Book of Life, but I will announce before my Father and his angels that they are mine.

> Revelation 3:4-5

Persevere, don't be indifferent.

Passionate relationship with God—that is what we are called to. Perseverance may sound good, sound doable, but to live it is not easy. For a day, for a week, maybe even a month, but to persevere over a long period is very difficult.

In our fast-paced society, the culture makes popular the ability to fall *in* love and *out* of love. Get married, and when you are not satisfied, upgrade your wife.

Relationship with God is characterized by marriage. It is being able to remain in a passionate relationship through the long haul, not when we feel good and when things are going well, but all regardless of the circumstances over the span of our lives, and with God for eternity. That is what these churches went through, and God is applauding some, while He is asking the others to come back to that relationship.

How about you? Are you standing strong in that relationship, or do you feel God calling you back? Return, persevere, love and remain.

#lovegod #beavailable #relationshipsmatter #makegodpriority #meaningfullife #letyourlifeshine #noreligion

Friday, September 27, 2013, New York, NY

461.

> Whenever the living beings give glory and honor
> and thanks to the one sitting on the throne (the
> one who lives forever and ever),

> Revelation 4:9

Worthy is the Lord.

I feel the passion of John as he envisions the One who sits on the throne. He's rambling on and on as he can to describe this wonderful vision. He sees the Lord is glorified, and he cannot but help in his excitement of seeing the One who is truly worthy to be praised. He cannot help but add more to claim his absolute agreement with what he is seeing.

And me too… I am excited to see the Lord be gloried, for He truly is worthy of all our praise and honor. I hope you do too.

#letmywordsbefew #renewal #heartmatters #worshipgod #sovereigngod

Saturday, September 28, 2013, New York, NY

462.

> But one of the twenty-four elders said to me, "Stop weeping! Look, the Lion of the tribe of Judah, the heir to David's throne, has won the victory. He is worthy to open the scroll and its seven seals."
>
> Revelation 5:5

Victory is already won.

There are times when we ruminate in our minds that we have failed in our lives, that we are ruined, that there is no opportunity for advancement and there is no hope for the future.

Yet, the truth remains, Jesus has already overcome for us! He is worthy of leading us, His people, to God. We can now have a direct relationship with God, and will be forever in His presence. God is good, and He has our future in His hands.

So, don't give up hope. Remain faithful. Know that the Lord is in control.

#sovereigngod #remaininhislove #trustgod #lookup #mygodissobig #godisfaithful #godlovesus #godisforus

Sunday, September 29, 2013, New York, NY

463.

> Then everyone - the kings of the earth, the
> rulers, the generals, the wealthy, the powerful,
> and every slave and free person - all hid
> themselves in the caves and among the rocks of
> the mountains. And they cried to the mountains
> and the rocks, "Fall on us and hide us from the
> face of the one who sits on the throne and from
> the wrath of the Lamb. For the great day of their
> wrath has come, and who is able to survive?"

Revelation 6:15-17

Great is our God.

Can there be times when we see God as small, as someone who would follow us and help us when we face problems?

Truth, He is a great God who obvious needs to follow no one. He is the great God, the One who can shake our senses and bring about great fear. Yet, we fail to understand the proper perspective of our position compared to our great God.

Fortunately, this great God is for us. So, whatever fears you may be going through in life, know that God is to be feared above all that. Rest in the truth that He is for us, and let us rest in His sovereignty.

#godisforus #sovereigngod #restwithgod #feargod #rightwithgod #blessingsfromgod #mygodissobig #lookup

Monday, September 30, 2013, New York, NY

464.

> After this I saw a vast crowd, too great to count,
> from every nation and tribe and people and
> language, standing in front of the throne and
> before the Lamb. They were clothed in white
> robes and held palm branches in their hands.
> And they were shouting with a great roar,
> "Salvation comes from our God who sits on the
> throne and from the Lamb!"

Revelation 7:9-10

The Church.

This is the picture of the Church. The crowd, the community, people of every nation, tribe, people, and language—that is the Church.

We often mistake the church to be a building, one with a name and an address, but the truth is that the Church is the people of God, or the bride of Jesus Christ.

We do not stand alone as individuals. We come together, and we are of Him. Our powerful groom, Jesus, leads us to purity.

How beautiful a picture of the Church, that we can stand before Him with a shout of how great He is. We can let go of all our worries, all our burdens and simply rely on the One who is the Salvation.

That day will come. Today, let us commit to perseverance and continual growth in knowing Him until then.

#makegodpriority #wearethechurch #hisgraceissufficient #renewal #lifetransformation #godusesregularpeople

Tuesday, October 1, 2013, New York, NY

465.

> When the Lamb broke the seventh seal on the
> scroll, there was silence throughout heaven for
> about half an hour.

Revelation 8:1

As bad things happen.

When the terrors on earth is happening . . . what would you do? When things go wrong in your life, work/school peers get you ruffled up, family members annoy us, things just don't go right, what would you do?

One thing many people do is to criticize God for allowing such things to happen, since He is in control, right? He allows such things to happen so that we may again learn to trust Him. He is able to get us out of difficulties if that is best for us, and will give us the ability to persevere through them otherwise.

When tribulation occurs, it is often a test of faith . . . it asks, will you still trust God despite these difficulties? So when things are difficult—trust Him more. Seek Him more. Lean on Him more. Don't be like those that go through the terrors of the tribulation and end up in hell away from God's presence because they turned away from God.

Trust in God, and walk with Him. He will certainly lead you.

#trustgod #walkwithgod #godhasaplan #godisfaithful #godisenough #godisourstrength #restwithgod #renewal

Wednesday, October 2, 2013, New York, NY

466.

> But the people who did not die in these plagues
> still refused to repent of their evil deeds and turn
> to God. They continued to worship demons and
> idols made of gold, silver, bronze, stone, and
> wood - idols that can neither see nor hear nor
> walk!

Revelation 9:20

Missing God's Glory.

Since there are many things going on in our lives—studies, work, projects, even church, family, and hobbies, we may lose the sight of God.

Revelation talks about some huge disasters and terrifying events where people should recognize that our God is great, but they still miss the big picture. They do not see who God is, and they continue on in their depraved ways.

How about us? Are we able to stop and see God's glory—His greatness and the weight of His presence despite the many things in our lives?

Don't miss what is more important than the things you may see around you.

People who don't know Jesus may not know or experience Him, but for us who have, let us remember to whom the glory belongs. Let us not live as if He is far away when He deserves the center of our attention.

#makegodpriority #worshipgod #turntogod #honorgod #narrowpath #bedifferent #letyourlifeshine #beavailable

Thursday, October 3, 2013, New York, NY

467.

> And the beast was allowed to wage war against God's holy people and to conquer them. And he was given authority to rule over every tribe and people and language and nation. Anyone who is destined for prison will be taken to prison. Anyone destined to die by the sword will die by the sword. This means that God's holy people must endure persecution patiently and remain faithful.
>
> Revelation 13:7,10

This is why there is suffering in this world. God allows it. It is because people who have faith in God are not worried about the pain and suffering here on earth, but looks forward to the eternal life that is ahead of us.

Satan can only manipulate things here on earth, and even then, for anything that is not in line with God's will, we can overcome them in the name of Jesus.

We do not need to fear, but rest in Jesus regardless of the calamity we face.

#nofear #restwithgod #godprovides #godisourstrength #godisenough #godisfaithful #noworries

Saturday, April 4, 2020, Old Tappan, NJ USA

468.

> "Fear God," he shouted. "Give glory to him. For the time has come when he will sit as judge. Worship him who made the heavens, the earth, the sea, and all the springs of water." This means that God's holy people must endure persecution patiently, obeying his commands and maintaining their faith in Jesus.
>
> Revelation 14:7,12

Going against the tide.

As the culture goes, it is all about us. We even demand that from the church. Instead of being a place of worship, the church has now become a place to get our egos boosted (and if not, the person would find another church).

This is also the trend of the views toward God—God serve me! (Well, if you don't, I may just not believe in You).

Let us remain against the culture and remain humble before the Lord. Though the world may turn away from God, this is where the believers of Jesus are to be faithful and persevere, for surely our Lord will protect us and save us.

Remain in Him. Stay strong!

#remaininhislove #noworries #wehaveallthatweneed #lookup #bedifferent #letyourlifeshine #noreligion

Tuesday, October 8, 2013, New York, NY

469.

> A mysterious name was written on her forehead:
> "Babylon the Great, Mother of All Prostitutes and
> Obscenities in the World."

Revelation 17:5

What do prostitutes mean in Scriptures?

Old Testament has many references to prostitutes and the same definition follows in Revelation. Prostitutes are people whose heart is not set on God (the groom). Opposite of prostitute would be the Church whose heart is fully devoted to the Lord.

Now, do people ever decide they want to be prostitutes in their future? No, it is at extended difficult situations that people may blame God, be stuck in worries (uncertainties of future), and lose their faith in God.

They may have believed in God at one point (the Church, or Christians collectively, marries Jesus who is the head and bridegroom of the Church), but when times became hard, and difficulties got prolonged, they turned away from God.

It was the bride/wife, but it has deserted their first love and went to another, or divorce has happened. It shows that we too may become prostitutes by turning away from God.

Let us be people of faith and stay close to the groom Jesus, through even the most difficult times that may even be prolonged.

#walkinfaith #remaininhislove #keepgoing #noreligion #notofthisworld #comeholyspirit #lovegod #waitongod

Wednesday, April 8, 2020, Old Tappan, NJ USA

470.

> The scarlet beast and his ten horns all hate the prostitute. They will strip her naked, eat her flesh, and burn her remains with fire. For God has put a plan into their minds, a plan that will carry out his purposes. They will agree to give their authority to the scarlet beast, and so the words of God will be fulfilled.

Revelation 17:16-17

Broken Unity.

God calls us to unity, one heart, and one direction. Just as He led people out of Egypt to the Promised Land, He desires us to be of one heart heading toward one direction. Yet, notice that the forces of evil are divided: they hate each other and they vie for power—we are not to be that way.

God was upset with the people who wanted to go back to Egypt, go their own ways, and serve other gods. And we too must be careful to not fall away.

Consider your heart attitudes toward other Christians. Are you able to follow as much as influence/lead? Is your life rooted in Scriptures and have a passionate desire to remain in Him?

Don't lose this battle. Jesus has already won the war. The battle is now for our hearts. Stay strong.

#loveothers #forgiveothers #heartmatters #relationshipsmatter #wearethechurch #letyourlifeshine #walkinfaith

Friday, October 11, 2013, New York, NY

471.

"How terrible, how terrible for that great city!
She was clothed in finest purple and scarlet
linens, decked out with gold and precious stones
and pearls! In a single moment all the wealth of
the city is gone!" And all the captains of the
merchant ships and their passengers and sailors
and crews will stand at a distance.

Revelation 18:16-17

Saving up for what matters.

When we do well and feel confident about what we have attained and are earning, we may place our trust in those things. As followers of Jesus Christ, let us not place our hearts on things that fade—money, properties, businesses, etc.

Rather, let us hold unswervingly to our God. Doing so will enable us to listen to His guidance and be obedient to it. The rewards received as a result is the eternal one, one that will not fade, rot, or disappear.

#trustgod #remaininhislove #wehaveallthatweneed #walkinfaith #notofthisworld #noworries #bedifferent

Saturday, October 12, 2013, New York, NY

472.

> Then I heard again what sounded like the shout
> of a vast crowd or the roar of mighty ocean
> waves or the crash of loud thunder: "Praise the
> LORD! For the Lord our God, the Almighty,
> reigns. Let us be glad and rejoice, and let us give
> honor to him. For the time has come for the
> wedding feast of the Lamb, and his bride has
> prepared herself.

Revelation 19:6-7

God who is worthy.

Have you ever been in such a state of anxiety because of the troubles that happen in life? Then as you prayed, God overwhelmed you and took all that fear away—let that be the baseline of our lives.

When worries come our way, troubles come. We know that just by experiencing God's sovereignty, His holiness, His awesomeness, His worthiness, and His presence, the weight of His glory—everything that we felt were important, difficult, fearful all disappear.

He is unchanging, unmoveable, and firm, and there is nothing that even comes close to His greatness.

So then, in the end, we will all be gathered together before Him. All the people from the least to the greatest—even those who do not turn to Him—will give praise to the Lord.

Let us recognize His worth now while we are still living, so that we may not be like those who will experience His wrath.

Our God is surely for us and wants the best for us. Let us draw close to Him, and worship Him as the One who is truly worthy.

#worshipgod #favorwithgod #restwithgod #walkwithgod #turntogod #lifetransformation #hisgraceissufficient

Sunday, October 13, 2013, New York, NY

474.

> And I saw a great white throne and the one sitting on it. The earth and sky fled from his presence, but they found no place to hide. I saw the dead, both great and small, standing before God's throne. And the books were opened, including the Book of Life. And the dead were judged according to what they had done, as recorded in the books.

Revelation 20:11-12

The war has been won.

Whatever circumstances you may be going through now, in the end, it all ends the same. The Holy God judges us, and the question comes down to whose team were you on? Jesus, or the world?

As we live our lives, let us consider the eternity. Many of us may feel there is so much to do, but there is so little time with your availability. We may rush from one task to another and perhaps even call it multi-tasking, while your mind is getting exhausted desiring to find rest.

When we think of eternal time, all these don't matter. We can take our time. What matters though, that the world will try to deceive us otherwise, is our relationship with God. Your faith in Jesus Christ assures you of your relationship, and the side on which you stand. Don't let the world drain your time and energy on doing what can be done in eternity—rather, focus on your relationship with God.

From time to time, drop everything and worship. Our war has been won, but the battle rages on from within our hearts. He desires all of us: our heart, our soul, our mind, and our strength.

So, remain til the end. Stay strong.

#comeholyspirit #noworries #remaininhislove #hisgraceissufficient #godprovides #godisenough #godisfaithful

Monday, October 14, 2013, New York, NY

475.

> Then I saw a new heaven and a new earth, for the old heaven and the old earth had disappeared. And the sea was also gone. And I saw the holy city, the new Jerusalem, coming down from God out of heaven like a bride beautifully dressed for her husband. I saw no temple in the city, for the Lord God Almighty and the Lamb are its temple. And the city has no need of sun or moon, for the glory of God illuminates the city, and the Lamb is its light.
>
> Revelation 21:1-2,22-23

New.

Life as we know it is not perfect. We have things to maintain such as credit card bills, cellphone bills, mortgages, rent, etc, and etc. Then there's difficulty at work, school, with friends, and sometimes even family. At times, we may regret life and wish things are not as they are.

The Good News points to something new. We can be renewed right now as the Spirit guides us, and shows us that our current pain is just temporary and that by following His guidance will lead us to the best in our present and future lives.

There is also a renewal of our lives at the end, where everything that hurt disappears, and the great, heavy, weighty presence of our glorious God is there and can be felt.

Everything we may be going through is temporary, so don't let those get you down. Instead, use those difficult times to draw closer to the Lord. This is in fact, where the Holy Spirit is leading us.

He is the only thing, the one thing, that matters.

#mygodissobig #noworries #trustgod #walkwithgod #worshipgod #waitongod #turntogod #comeholyspirit

Tuesday, October 15, 2013, New York, NY

476.

> Let the one who is doing harm continue to do harm; let the one who is vile continue to be vile; let the one who is righteous continue to live righteously; let the one who is holy continue to be holy." Blessed are those who wash their robes. They will be permitted to enter through the gates of the city and eat the fruit from the tree of life. The Spirit and the bride say, "Come." Let anyone who hears this say, "Come." Let anyone who is thirsty come. Let anyone who desires drink freely from the water of life.
>
> Revelation 22:11,14,17

Reading verse 11, I began to wonder, where do I fit in?

Could I be the one who does harm, the one who is vile, the one who is righteous, or the one who is holy?

Then began my thoughts about my shortcomings of matching the holiness of our God. When I think about righteousness, that is being right with God and others, I surely fail in many places and do not measure up.

Fortunately, the Gospel of grace simply says to come, and He will wash off our filth and enable us to be holy and righteous simply because of who He is, and what He has done.

Verse 17 is so comforting: we just need to come, and we can come thirsty—and He will fill us with water of life.

#letgoletgod #hisgraceissufficient #renewal #godisenough #comeaayouare #restwithgod #noworries

Wednesday, October 16, 2013, New York, NY

Hashtags (topics) Count

#trustgod	216		#noreligion	31
#letyourlifeshine	133		#narrowpath	30
#bedifferent	84		#comeholyspirit	29
#calling	82		#mygodissobig	29
#listentogod	79		#godisourstrength	28
#wearethechurch	77		#blessingsfromgod	27
#godhasaplan	76		#renewal	27
#letgoletgod	73		#bemerciful	26
#godisforus	71		#expectfromgod	26
#walkwithgod	66		#befruitful	25
#godprovides	65		#meaningfullife	25
#loveothers	65		#restwithgod	25
#makegodpriority	65		#keepgoing	24
#hisgraceissufficient	64		#sovereigngod	24
#heartmatters	62		#bethereforoneanother	23
#gowhengodcalls	59		#godisable	23
#honorgod	57		#noworries	23
#wehaveallthatweneed	56		#nofear	22
#walkinfaith	52		#breakthrough	20
#lookup	51		#godlovesus	19
#bethankful	49		#givetoothers	18
#blessothers	49		#godusesregularpeople	18
#obeygod	49		#favorwithgod	17
#godisenough	47		#godrestores	17
#turntogod	43		#nothingisimpossiblewithgod	17
#abandonall	42		#worshipgod	17
#feargod	42		#godforgives	15
#notofthisworld	42		#pray	15
#remaininhislove	41		#rightwithgod	15
#lovegod	35		#letmywordsbefew	14
#pathsstraight	35		#loveconquersall	12
#visionary	35		#weareforgivenandfree	10
#lifetransformation	34		#beavailable	9
#waitongod	33		#comeasyouare	7
#relationshipsmatter	32		#godcorrects	7
#submittogod	32		#onefamily	6
#godisfaithful	31		#forgiveothers	5

Dr. Sang Sur is the founder of Prayer Tents, a Christian mission organization that seeks to enable people to find life by meeting Jesus through relationships with Christians near them. He is called to bi-vocational ministry, being a tentmaker as he works with other business leaders to bring many to Christ, while also giving support to the global Church.

Sang is the chief executive officer of Sciturus Real Investment Group, along with its sister companies Hanmaum Realty and Techellence. He is an engineering and business executive who led technology M&A that resulted in $53 million in revenue growth of two major global-reaching companies within the first year. He also directed personnel across all functions of engineering in modernizing aeronautical radar and countermeasure systems that continue to prevent US C-130s and B-52s from being shot down in hostile territories. As an Air Force officer, he was part of the Air Force Special Operations Command, ensuring the best aerial equipment for the US military, particularly the Special Forces. He holds a Ph.D. in Business Administration and Management and two doctorates in fields of ministry (Th.D. and D.Min.).

Sang is also an ordained Christian pastor and a Certified Executive Coach, and he works with Christian executives in the marketplace and with pastors to enable them to go beyond their perceived limits and fulfill their great callings from God. Sang is a member of the Christian Business Men's Connection (CBMC) and chairs the NYC group.

Sang lives in New Jersey with his wife, son, and daughter.

Find out more about him at www.sangsur.com.

Our Highest Calling

A new book from Dr. Sang Sur

Make disciples of all nations as
you are going, baptizing,
and teaching.

Matthew 28:19-20

The Great Commission
is a way of life. It is something
to be carried out as one is
going about. It is not a one-
time evangelistic event. It is a
call to make disciples as we live
out our lives.

In our modern day, Christians have fallen prey to the trends of
the world, including idolizing busyness and individualism, which are
counter to the love that God called us to share and the community we
are to be. The center of focus of the Early Church was love toward God
and others, which fulfilled the Greatest Commandment.

Our Highest Calling is about how to live out that life, and it is
through discipleship that we can make disciples in our lives. Discipleship
is a practice of love with other close-knit Christian brothers and sisters
over time. It is about being available for one another and pursuing God-
given callings together for the kingdom of God. As Christians grow in
discipleship and form deep relationships, they will in turn make disciples
who truly love God. They can then walk together and make even more
disciples, just as Jesus and His disciples did throughout their lives.

Interact with other readers and find out more at

ourhighestcalling.com

Did you like the reflections you read?

You can stay up to date with Dr. Sur's Scripture reflections at prayertents.com. He shares his thoughts publicly as he shares with his small group. Just find him and subscribe to His posts.

We encourage you to do the same kind of reflections and write them down.

In fact, we encourage you to do this in a small group with other close Christian brothers or sisters. Reflect on Scriptures together and share how it relates to your life with one another. Doing so will both deepen your relationships and enable you to grow together as disciples of Jesus.

www.ingramcontent.com/pod-product-compliance
Lightning Source LLC
Chambersburg PA
CBHW031511120626
46545CB00005B/1835